MINDSETMAKEOVER

The

Resilient

Leader

Energize your leadership

Cynthia Howard RN, PHD, LSSBB

Copyright © 2022 Cynthia Howard RN, PhD, LSSBB

ISBN: 978-0-578-45444-3

Cover design by Todd Siatkowsky, Special Forces Art Department

All rights reserved. No part of this book may be reproduced or transmitted in any form or by any means, electronic or mechanical, including photocopying, recording or by any information storage and retrieval system without written permission of the publisher, except for the inclusion of brief quotations in a review.

Printed in the United States of America

TABLE OF CONTENTS

Why This Book Matters 8

Chapter 1 Your Capacity to Perform (Hint: It's Resilience) 14

Resilient Leaders Do the Following Differently 19

    Three Myths That Get in the Way of Activating Your Resilience 21

You Under Pressure 24

Chapter 2 The Elephant in the Room 29

It is not what you do, but how you do it................................35

3 Mindset Shifts that Matter 37

    Mindset Shift #1: How You Feel (Awareness) 38

    Mindset Shift #2: How You Think (Anticipate) 44

    Mindset Shift #3: What You Do (Agile) 50

Chapter Overview..54

Chapter Summary: The Elephant in the Room.................56

Study Group Activity 57

Chapter 3 Beyond Self-Doubt and Bias: Mindset Distortions 59

Perfectionism..62

Bias: Mindset Distortion..67

Chapter Summary: Beyond Fear and Bias........................74

Study Group Activity 75

Chapter 4 Habits: For Better or Worse.... 76

Infrastructure Habits (The Habits to Build On)................82

From Autopilot to Power Mindset...............86

Chapter Summary: Habits...............88

Study Group Activity...............89

Chapter 5 Why Can't I Get Anything Done at Work? 90

Common Energy Drains at Work...............92

    There Is Never Enough Time...............93

    Most Plans Fail - Why?...............97

    Why Goals Fail to Engage...............100

    Too Much to Do and a Lack of Priorities...............103

    Status Quo...............115

    Office Politics...............117

Managing Expectations (Setting Boundaries)...............122

    Managing Others' Expectations...............124

Boundaries...............127

    Boundary Quiz: How Well Do You Set Boundaries?...............128

A Toxic Workplace (and Ten Signs of a Healthy One)...............130

    Seven Signs of a Toxic Workplace...............132

    Ten Signs of a Healthy Workplace...............134

Chapter Summary: Why Can't I Get Anything Done at Work?...............135

Study Group Activity...............136

Chapter 6 Emotional Agility...............138

Optimism: A Precursor to Resilient Thinking...............146

Emotions Are Part of Your Survival Kit...............149

    Emotional Hijacking (The Runaway Stress Reaction)...............151

Emotional Awareness (Name It and Tame It)...............153

    Fatal Emotions...............161

Chapter Summary: Emotional Intelligence *167*

Study Group Activity *168*

Chapter 7 Resilient Thinking 170

You Are the Message *173*

    Reflection 175

Resilient Mindset: Check Yourself *176*

Chapter 8 Strategies to Activate Resilience 179

Breathing Techniques *180*

Manage Your Energy. Increase Your Time. *182*

Take a Moment (3-Second Transition) *183*

    Homework 185

Mindful Attention *186*

    Reduce Emotional Hijacking and Runaway Stress Reactions 192

    The Body Scan: Quick Check-In 196

Journaling *198*

Chapter Summary: Mindset Reboot *203*

Study Group Activity *204*

Appendix 205

5 Why's *206*

Interruption Log *208*

Perfectionism Self Check & 360 .... *209*

16 Dimensions on the EQi 2.0 .... *210*

Mindful Attention Worksheet *213*

The Work Smart Club Network 214

About Work Smart Consulting 215

About the Author 216
Other Books Written by Dr. Cynthia Howard 217
References 218
Endnotes 223

You cannot outperform your capacity.

Today's world of distraction drains capacity unless you have a strategy to activate your resilience.

Why This Book Matters

Change fatigue. Decision fatigue. Can you and your organization keep up with the pace of change?

Research shows most leaders (and organizations) are not keeping up with the demands of this digital age: the accelerated pace of change, relentless demands for value, resignations, multigenerational workforce, regulators, and the list goes on.

How do you lead teams who are resistant, tired, and disengaged? Their heads are spinning from another change effort that reorganizes their job—and your head may be spinning from having to execute it.

According to studies, 84% of change efforts fail due to poor planning and execution. However, it is not for lack of trying or effort. In my own practice, I work with leaders who are saddled with the pressure of trying to roll the boulder uphill, only to find they are on the wrong hill.

Let's face it, the nature of pressure is to eventually blow up. The choice today seems like you can explode—for everyone to see—or implode, silently bearing the pain of failure and disappointment, wondering how you could have done better. Either way, the experience can cause profound damage that carries personal risk to health, one's future potential, as well as damage to the organization. This is a lose-lose scenario.

Organizations do not need additional policies, procedures, strategic plans, or flow charts. What they need are passionate, creative, and engaged leaders. This sets the tone for everyone else.

Results really matter, and the way to get better results is to build your capacity as a leader. But in order to stop pushing the same boulder up the wrong hill, you need a mindset shift.

Technology has changed how we live, communicate, and work, yet leaders continue to relate to their teams and organize their companies as if living in the past. The digital age has arrived. More information will be produced this year than in the past five thousand years.

This requires a leader who is energized, engaged, and present to take on this challenge. Leaders need to be bolder than ever to have the same impact they used to have. They must be emotionally equipped to get and keep their team's attention. Inspiration doesn't come from the procedure manual; it comes from leaders who share their passion and purpose for why this particular job is going to make a difference in the world.

This can only happen when leaders recognize that their power and ability to influence comes from who they are as human beings, not their positions or titles.

The skills needed to run a department are different from the skills needed to lead through change. This is the elephant in the room that I want to address and help you move beyond.

As an executive coach for the past twenty years, I have worked with thousands of leaders, professionals, and business owners. I have heard the same complaints about the same issues over and over and have seen patterns and problems with the execution of ideas and plans.

Distractions are the new normal, and focus is almost nonexistent. The average attention span is eight seconds. How well can the stated outcomes of organizations—*speed, quality, value, and sustainable growth*—be executed with a distracted mindset?

Consider the following elements of performance: ability and expertise, purpose and reward, motivation and interest, state of mind, team members, and style and approach. Did you know that out of those traits, state of mind contributes 50% of the variation in performance?[1] Yet, less than 5% of training is devoted to mindset.

Think about your own situation: how much of your time and resources do you devote to developing your mindset? The way you think dictates what you do and how you show up. As the leader, how you show up influences how your team shows up and is what drives the performance engine.

Showing up—always on, always at your best—is quite the challenge, especially today when most have greater intimacy with technology than with each other (on average, people look at their phones 150 times a day). How can a leader have the needed impact, engage their followers, and get things done in a 24/7, always-on world?

It is with a resilient mindset. This is the capacity to be your best while dealing with the unexpected. This book offers three major mindset shifts you can make to develop your resilient mindset along with strategies to be more effective.

As a pioneer of resilient thinking, I recognized that leaders who learned to thrive did so because they learned to manage their energy. They were self-aware, exhibited self-control, had grit, and were optimistic, flexible, and confident. This enabled them to think differently about the challenges they faced.

How you think matters, and how you think about *yourself* matters the most because this sets everything in motion. Are you self-aware? Do you have authentic confidence, enabling the impact and influence you need? Do you have the stamina and grit to anticipate resistance and lead through it?

Or do you avoid challenges, conflicts, and demands, fearing you won't be able to handle it? Or worse, do you think that what worked in the past is the best approach today, even though everything has changed (it worked then; it should work now)?

This book is filled with practical tools. Use them and engage your teams with them. The tools are the milestones along the road to help you make the three mindset shifts to build your resilient mindset.

As you read the book, step back, take a deep breath, and think about *your* thinking. Ask yourself, "Am I aware of what I am feeling? Do I anticipate change, or do I react? Am I agile, flexible? How well do I adapt? Do I need a mindset makeover?"

These are a few questions to consider as you energize your leadership. How do you eat that elephant? One bite at a time. Let's go.

Above all else, guard your heart, for everything you do flows from it.

— Proverbs 4:23

Chapter 1
Your Capacity to Perform (Hint: It's Resilience)

Technology has changed how we live, work, and communicate. Researchers say people interact with their phones 150 times a day—this is more intimacy with devices than with people. Thirteen hours a week is spent on email, and screen time can take up to eight hours of the day.

Texting, emojis, and abbreviations have replaced face-to-face communication. This constant flow of distractions has created a false sense of urgency.

Most people are walking around with some uncertainty, anxiety, and reactivity.

Think about it: there will always be 24 hours in a day. Time is finite. How do some people get so much done and others have a long list of unfinished projects, finding it difficult to get through the day? People who get things done have learned to manage their energy and stop the leaks. This increases their capacity to go beyond burnout and accomplish more without working longer or harder.

Resilience is capacity. It is your ability to bounce—forward. This may be the most important set of skills you have never been taught!

Leaders today have to learn to thrive in uncertainty without sacrificing their energy and motivation.

Tune into your capacity, every day. You have to replace the energy you use on a regular basis.

Most people forget that to achieve their goals, they must expand their capacity to take on new and bigger challenges. And they need a surplus of energy along the way.

Having seen many successful leaders short circuit their potential, sacrifice their personal lives, or opt out of the game, I wanted to provide a roadmap with a proven approach to getting it done without sacrificing your potential in the process. We have proven strategies in Chapter 8 to stop the energy leaks that destroy your capacity and erode confidence, presence, and effectiveness.

Living in the digital age is amazing. In airports, stores, and offices, there are charging stations for your devices—and even your car—but there aren't any charging stations for you. If you want to stop leaking energy and learn to recharge so you can go beyond where you are now and achieve your dreams, then you need a strategy and a mindset that will carry you through.

Organizational change is two-dimensional: if you want your organization to change – you have to change first!

Your personal engagement and willingness to change how you communicate, lead, and manage your work is what makes change successful—or not.

When planning a new initiative or some type of change – get clear with how you must change first. Communicate this to you team and you will quickly get buy-in.

To illustrate this point, let me share the story of an informal leader that made a big difference in her organization. I met Lisa during a project I was working on with a major healthcare system. I was hired to provide training and consulting around conflict and collaboration skills. Departments were being restructured and people that had been in their roles for quite some time were being put on different teams.

Needless to say, there was tension. Lisa was a Clinical Specialist and worked with the team providing education and clinical support. She did not have direct management authority or responsibility.

She described it this way: "I have worked here for 10 years, and I know everyone that is being restructured. They trust me. So, when I heard their complaints and saw how stressed they were, I wanted to do something."

The healthcare system was also in the midst of their annual health drive encouraging employees to adopt healthier habits. Lisa said, "I personally had decided to start walking more and had a lightbulb moment. What if I organized a walking group? I approached the people who just went through this restructuring and suggested we all walk together 3 times a week. It fit with the hospital wide 10K Steps program and brought everyone together a couple of times a week. They could still check in with each other, blow off some of that pent-up stress and help them make the transition."

Successful leadership is the ability to influence the informal structure within the organization. Lisa found a way to channel her care into an effective solution. This ended up being a win-win-win because the director of the department implemented "walking meetings" getting people out of the department and refreshing the meeting format. It also energized everyone.

How the team shows up is a reflection of how the leader shows up. Be the leader regardless of your formal title. If you have the trust of the group, engage everyone to work toward the desired goal.

Your impact depends on your awareness. Be curious about the possibility in the challenge; otherwise, you may end up acting in the same worn-out way you have always acted.

As you go through the day, do you recognize the worker giving 150%, or do you ignore their efforts and move along, distracted by other problems?

A resilient mindset is essential because:

- » There is little downtime between challenges.
- » To be successful, you must perform at a higher standard.
- » No one will save you.
- » This life is yours now. There is no do-over.
- » It is critical to manage your emotions so you will not be managed *by* them.
- » Because going back to the "way it used to be" is not an option.

What has stress, pressure, and constant busyness cost you? (Relationships, promotions, opportunity, day-to-day peace?)

Take a moment and think about what you have missed or sacrificed due to stress. Write it out in your journal.

Resilient Leaders Do the Following Differently

1. They do not shy away from challenge. They can accept the reality of the challenge and set out to find a plan to deal with it.

2. They find meaning in the challenge. Those engaging a resilient mindset recognize that the biggest challenges often help them develop their greatest assets. By finding meaning in hardship, they can build a bridge from what seems like a setback to new possibility.

3. They learn to laugh at themselves. Resilient people do not take themselves seriously; they can find the humor in their mistakes or their challenges.

4. They learn to improvise. When faced with a challenge, it is important to be flexible and adapt. Everyone faces difficult times—either through divorce, a changing job market or restructuring. Resilient people will continue to do what it takes to keep going.

5. They practice strategies to protect themselves from the distraction (and destruction) of stress. Mindfulness, visualization, and breathing techniques have been used by Olympic athletes, performers, and other successful people in their efforts to keep going.

6. They learn to embrace uncertainty, adapt, be flexible, and learn from their challenges. Rather than resist what is happening and burn up valuable energy reserves, resilience enables them to keep moving forward.

7. They are self-aware. Knowing what is going on internally is valuable. This increases your awareness of what is happening in others, also.

Out of the seven, what do you do well? And what do you need to do more often? Highlight or make a note next to each one to remind you of what needs your focus.

The thinking that got you to this point is not the thinking that will move you to the next level.

Keep in mind, being resilient doesn't mean you do not experience any distress; it means you keep going despite the challenges because you have learned to think differently as a result of it.

It is a mindset.

Three Myths That Get in the Way of Activating Your Resilience

1. "I work best under pressure."

The stress reaction is a hardwired reaction that has been part of our nervous system for the last 100,000 years. Once this flight, fight, or freeze reaction is engaged, then rational, logical, and critical thinking is suspended. This reaction is emotional in nature and obliterates creative problem solving.

This primitive reaction is engaged more easily as technology takes over our attention and the day is hijacked by an endless stream of distractions. Many people are stuck in the throes of this reaction, not realizing what has happened to their attention.

Over 95% of the choices people make during the day are made on autopilot. This means that choices are reactive; the focus is on what is most urgent instead of most important, and this urgency drives decisions.

When you tell yourself there is never enough time or resources, it is easy to procrastinate or feel resentful or angry. This can set up a chain reaction of other feelings of being a victim and powerless. First, you need to recognize you are operating on autopilot and shift into a mindful and aware state.

How tuned in are you to what is happening around you and the impact on you? When you are caught in a chronic stress reaction, most people make decisions in the moment without fully evaluating their feelings, where the feelings are coming from and the consequences of reacting.

Procrastination is a default mode for people who tell themselves they work best under pressure. Putting things off and never finishing anything can be one way to stay a step ahead of feeling the pressure. If this is something you tell yourself, acknowledge the myth and break out of this pattern.

2. "You can never be too prepared."

Are you overpreparing because you do not feel capable? Do you lack clarity on the desired outcome? Are you stuck in paralysis by analysis?

The Imposter Syndrome was identified decades ago, and this is one of the symptoms[6]. The Imposter Syndrome is when you never feel confident despite your accomplishments. You can see how overpreparing seems like a rational way to establish confidence. Unfortunately, it sabotages it!

Create an inventory of your strengths and learn to own them. This is one of the ways you will avert this irrational fear of being found out as a fraud.

Problem solving—under pressure—is one of the dimensions in emotional intelligence. It is being able to clearly define the problem and work through the process of solving it. Having a standardized problem-solving process like DMAIC or Plan-Do-Check-Act will keep you informed and clear.

3. "You can never think too much about a problem."

This sounds like justification for analysis paralysis and ruminating about problems.

Overthinking is like overpreparing. It short circuits resilience. Why? It is based on fear of not being good enough and does not let go of the past. Science shows us that those people who can move on from what happened in the past demonstrate a resilient mindset.

Good thinking solves problems and prevents unnecessary new ones.

You need good input in order to have creative solutions, so make it a habit to challenge your assumptions and conclusions. Use a standardized problem-solving process. Give yourself time in your schedule to think; go through all aspects of the problem and its solutions. Imagine productive and successful scenarios.

This is not the same thing as worrying.

Overthinking and worry are not strategies to handle pressure. They are the default for a stress reaction gone wild. Chronic stress reduces the ability to think clearly and broadly, instead keeping you focused on a small area. Here is where trying too hard only gets in the way of clear, focused problem-solving and decisions.

If you are feeling worried or fearful, you are overly focused on the problem. Keep your eye on solutions, and you will be more energized.

You Under Pressure

How has stress, tension and distraction affected your ability to lead, think clearly make good decisions? Has it impacted your ability to love, care for, and communicate with your family, friends, or partner?

Aside from the many negative side effects of the stress reaction, the most consequential is that it can quickly isolate people. The very resource (relationships) that renews and recharges one's energy is gone.

Some people decide work is their most important relationship—sacrificing personal fulfillment—while others try to be everything it everyone; either way, there is no balance.

The stress reaction changes how you think, make decisions, and learn. Your higher functions in your brain are unhooked when in the stress reaction. You may get stuck in rumination or overthinking.

Overthinking takes your personality hostage.
You are now showing up with most of your internal resources shut down.

Chronic pressure sets up a cycle of overthinking and this can lead to micromanaging or the opposite, abdicating decisions and letting "everything work itself out."

Whether you are managing people to achieve the next goal, finding common ground with your teenagers, or spending time with your partner, you need the capacity to manage conflicting demands and bring it all together. This is hard to do when you have your own internal conflicts draining your energy and distracting you.

How do you handle a negative employee, a critical boss, or an upset spouse when you are distracted with your own personal issues, with deadlines looming and pressures mounting?

Unless you have tools, are self-aware, and can self-regulate, you'll probably end up over- or underreacting, making the situation worse.

Can you see how important it is to manage yourself first in order to make an impact at work, in your business, and at home?

Every day, both at work and at home, you make decisions about how you will perform based, in part, on your internal drivers. Are you inspired to be a part of the problem-solving effort, or are you part of the problem? Whatever you decide, a chain reaction is set into motion, affecting how you feel about yourself and how you respond to others.

It is a myth that one can leave emotions "at home." You do not go through your day having a neutral impact on the world around you.

You are not invisible. Whether you recognize the impact or not, you are influencing your world. Is it the impact you want to have?

Do you notice when you cross the line between performance and pressure?

Look at the chart on the next page[7]

The top line represents you, with your resilience activated, able to sustain your performance. The bottom line is what happens to you and your performance with unchecked stress.

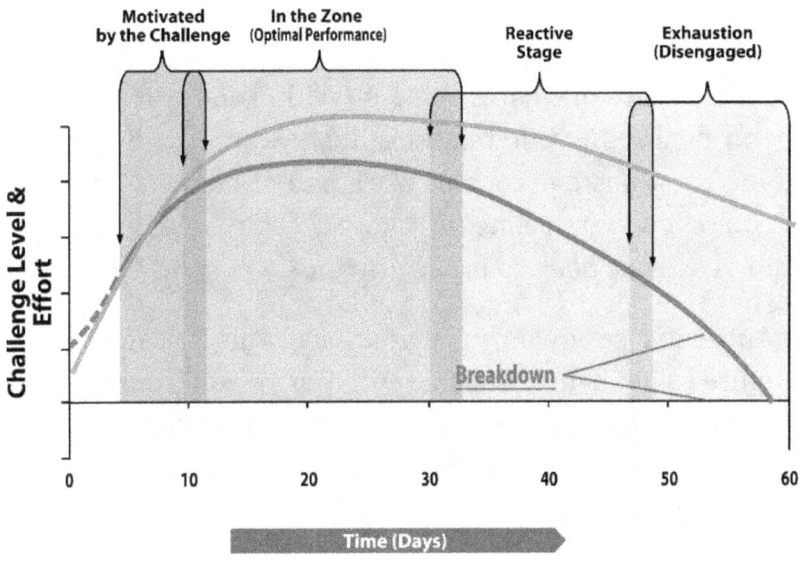

Emotions are contagious. Science knows through the mirror neuron system that our brains match what we see in others. When distracted and under pressure, the stress reaction is triggered, and one goes into survival mode. This "vibe" is picked up by everyone around you who is likely to mirror your tone, gestures, and even mood.

It's hard to build trust when you are distracted by your inner demands. When I talk with leaders, people problems and relationship issues are what keeps them up at night. Whether it is the negative or needy employee, staff who hate you, the colleague who is trying to sabotage you, or the many other distractions from staff and peers who want you to solve everything, people problems will make or break your day.

Being aware of what is going on within you will help you deal with your relationships. Awareness helps you set a positive tone at work and at home. When you show up feeling in charge, your confidence increases, as does your performance.

Authentic is showing up at your best. This is so much more than being transparent. When you connect more often, in a genuine and sincere way, you will enjoy your relationships more and recharge your battery.

Chapter 2
The Elephant in the Room

"I can't get anything to stick. How do I get my team to follow through on what I want?"

I met Melanie at a networking event, and when she found out what I did, she blurted out her frustration. We found a quiet place to talk, and she went on to explain.

"This department has consistently underperformed. I even hired a new director to provide more oversight to the department, but I ended up firing him at his 90-

day review. The team complained about him constantly, even though I really got along with him and thought we worked well together. I have wasted six months in this process. My CEO is not going to be happy with me, and I am not happy with my team. We are starting over—again."

Unfortunately, Melanie's frustration is all too common: not getting commitment from the team, misreading the real problem, and hiring the wrong people for the job. Melanie saw it differently: "Nothing I do pleases this team." She didn't fully understand the challenges her team was facing and the type of leader they would need to build trust and work through their challenges. The most important thing to her was how well she would get along with the director. All those conflicts add up quickly, not to mention the more subtle problems at play, like the expectations of the company's leadership model, silos, and culture.

Melanie had a long list of issues to discuss, but she couldn't tell me what the *team* thought the problem was; she had not explored that with them. She was basing her information on what she'd gleaned from the department manager, who used the same talking points: "You can't please the team." Clearly, they had developed a dead-end feedback loop, an echo chamber that failed to expand the understanding of the situation at hand.

This is one of the elephants in the room: failed communication and the absence of a system to ensure information is continually flowing.

Many organizations have a revolving door and struggle with retention, engagement, and employee stress. According to Gallup, employee engagement has remained around 33% for the past decade, despite the millions of dollars spent on engagement programs.

Here are some of the findings from a recent Gallup survey[2]:

- » 51% of workers are looking for a new job.

- » 79% go to work without any guidance on how well—or how poorly—they are doing their job.

- » 70% of the workforce wants feedback on how they are doing.

- » 88% indicate they had a terrible onboarding process.

What does this data show? "Work" is not working—for staff or for leaders.

It's time to think differently - about how you lead and work.

Many leaders burn out within 18 months, barely enough time to learn the job. Why are employees more burned out than ever before? Why is workplace stress at an all-time high? Why are we still struggling with employee retention? Where are all the new leaders to replace the ones who leave?

There's a big fat elephant in the room—"elephants" being the issues that get bigger and heavier the longer they're ignored. These elephants are costing you time, money, and skilled talent. And sometimes, you don't even realize they are there.

This includes the elephants that challenge a common mindset in leaders: "This is the way we have always done it here."

This elephant may come in the form of a leader not picking up on the needs of the team. It could be her lack of communication skills or the flurry of daily activity that gets in the way of the "real" work that advances the team's strategic goals.

Confusion and chaos in the workplace compete for everyone's attention and effort, taking energy and focus necessary to get the *real* work done that advances the strategic goals.

70% of initiatives fail. People miss deadlines, go overbudget, or scrap the project altogether. Even with the framework of continuous improvement and agile lean sigma, workers fail to deliver on initiatives. They run into delays, overrun costs, and fail to disrupt the status quo. Essentially, nothing changes, despite massive effort, resources, and energy devoted to the project.

I was once working with a VP of Patient Care Services who was so frustrated, she was ready to leave a lucrative position just to find some relief. Fortunately, she hired me as her executive coach. Several of her departments were coming in with very low satisfaction scores. Other key performance indicators were also underperforming.

She explained, "Six months ago, I hired a company to do a major training on patient experience. I had all the department heads and frontline staff attend. It was a major effort to coordinate, pay for staff to stay over, and provide staff to fill in. We hadn't even gotten the next quarter results in yet, and I heard the CFO cancelled the project. I was not part of that decision."

Her frustration was clear: "This hit me right in my gut. I am not sure why I keep working so hard."

The backstory in this situation is that there were several "patient experience" projects going on. The CFO made the decision without exploring or discussing it with anyone outside of the executive team. The VP also had not openly discussed the problem with her leadership team. The pattern of not talking was part of the culture.

This was a missed opportunity for the entire department. Problems are excellent opportunities to talk about what is going on. Instead of transforming the patient experience, staff ended up confused from the mixed messages and leaders felt demoralized.

In today's "always on" world, there never seems to be enough time. This false sense of urgency compels leaders to compromise on their problem-solving approach, jumping to solutions at epidemic rates. And even with the proven methods of agile lean sigma, leaders still tend to compromise on the approach, which then affects results.

How do you approach problems? Are they an opportunity to learn? Or something to quickly get through?

I help you find that elephant and deal with it.

Because at the end of the day, a new degree or more technical skills won't help you solve these problems. It's your ability to react to what is happening, to have the difficult conversations, and to stop walking past the elephant in the room with your eyes closed, hoping it will go away.

Elephants don't go away.

But they are easier to handle than you might think.

That's my job: to help you eat the elephant, one bite at a time.

If you are reacting instead of enacting—jumping to solutions rather than gathering information and using a problem-solving approach—this book will help you reboot your mindset. You have an opportunity right now to make small adjustments that will unlock your potential to influence, persuade, and lead.

It is not what you do, but how you do it.

I want to introduce you to Kelly Johnson. In 1943, he and his secret team designed, built, and launched "America's first operational jet fighter," the P-80, in less than 150 days! That's right. From concept to takeoff, they swiftly completed the aircraft. Later, he continued to amaze the world with other projects, including the Lockheed U-2 spy plane, created and built in less than nine months.

His team, nicknamed "Skunk Works," had an apt motto: "boldly innovate." Kelly Johnson's guiding principle was "small, empowered teams create powerful solutions." To achieve such dramatic accomplishments, Kelly handpicked a small team of engineers based on the expertise needed in each project. They worked offsite, away from distractions. He operated under 14 rules of management, which is still up on Lockheed Martin's website.

Johnson outlined an operational system that kept the teams small and reports to a minimum. He emphasized "important work recorded thoroughly," clearly spelling out roles and responsibilities, including a reward system based on results. His main requirement was flexibility, which he felt was essential in order to achieve the desired results.

How much of what you are doing is for an arbitrary reason? How committed are you to comply when you do not see the relevance? How do you think your team feels when they struggle with other daily hassles that are not contributing to progress?

Here is another dramatic real-world comparison. Have you heard of the Las Vegas Harmon Hotel project from 2014? It was the most expensive billboard—oh, I mean *hotel*—in Las Vegas. It never opened, eventually standing 26 stories high (short of the proposed 49 stories) and only used to hang advertising banners.

It started with a dream team of the *best* architects, engineers, builders, and contractors that money could buy. Unfortunately, construction issues, legal troubles, and engineering snafus meant the hotel never opened. It was built on a fault line and would topple in an earthquake. It was ultimately dismantled.

The team cited "communication issues" as a primary reason for the failures. How can this happen when you have renowned experts on your team, including those in the construction industry who deal with earthquakes for a living? The project was problematic from the beginning.

Compare this to a different hotel. In 2011, the Broad Sustainable Building company in China put up a 30-story hotel in 15 days. You can see the time lapse video on YouTube.

How is this possible? Very simply, the founder of this company approached the project from a different perspective than the dream team in Las Vegas. He recognized there were problems in traditional construction and looked at building this hotel with a new set of eyes.

It is not what you do, but how you do it.

To do something differently, you have to first think differently about your problems and how to approach them. You need a mindset makeover.

3 Mindset Shifts that Matter

Can we all agree *unexpected challenges* have taken over the workday and obscured *urgent* and *important*, producing frantic deadlines on a never ending "to-do" list? This drains precious energy and momentum from your ability to do your job and your team's ability to focus. Important work does not get done, yet everyone is always busy.

This distraction triggers an underlying stress reaction and distorts what you feel, think and do.

These are the three mindset shifts that will transform your effectiveness and your sense of satisfaction.

Whether you are an executive or entry-level, a formal leader or aspiring leader, keep an open mind as you read though the three mindset makeovers that matter most.

Mindset Shift #1: How You Feel (Awareness)

Being self-aware is knowing what is going on inside of you, and how it will impact the outcome (your performance). The greater your self-awareness, the greater your situational awareness.

Think about your car; you get oil changes because the engine does best with fresh, clean and sufficient oil. You check the oil light and tune into the dashboard to make sure temperature, pressure, and gas are all within desired range. Humans, however, do not have an obvious dashboard – emotions are usually the first indicator there is a problem, and emotions get ignored. By nature, we lack self-awareness. Most ignore the warning lights on their personal dashboard.

This mindset shift has to do with what you feel. Too often feelings are ignored. This becomes a major elephant – something that gets bigger and heavier because it is ignored. Knowing what you are feeling is going to help you take the right action.

Logically, it makes sense that when you can control something you can make needed adjustments. Same is true when you control your attention and tune into your emotions, thoughts and attitude; you can flex as needed to achieve the desired outcome. Self-awareness is you acknowledging the impact of your emotions on decisions, interactions and how you show up.

Research shows a corrrelation between emotional awareness and performance; over ninety percent of leaders that exhibited high levels of self-awareness had high performing teams. And the opposite is true, leaders with low levels of self-awareness created a toxic culture seventy eight percent of the time.[3]

Being self-aware is a strong predictor of success. It is cited most often as a characteristic of effective leaders. Monitoring emotions, thoughts, and actions, and then fine tuning those emotions and thoughts gives the leader an edge. It also has been shown to deepen personal satisfaction, increase situational awareness, along with compassion and empathy demonstrated to others.

Great, self-awareness will make a leader happier and more effective! But why is this so difficult?

You may not realize that most of the time you are going through the day on autopilot. The brain's main goal is to conserve resources and be efficient, your mind develops habits in thinking and emotions to save time and energy. This becomes your mindset. The default mode is to go through the day unaware of what you are thinking and how you feel. This is a big reason to develop self-awareness.

In addition, the brain has bias and distortions hardwired into the thinking process, and when you add in distraction and the stress reaction, higher thinking functions are disabled. (We cover bias in Chapter 4.)

Basically, it is not natural to tune into oneself. However, as any golfer, musician, Olympic athlete and performer knows, **you have to tune in if you want to turn on your potential.**

Super Tip:

Think about the feedback you receive from others; does it match your view of how you show up? If not, you would benefit from increasing self-awareness.

Unfortunately, executives and many leaders operate in an echo chamber and miss out on feedback. You can use a 360-type assessment and see if there is a gap in how you think you show up and how others rate you.

The most significant contributor to performance variation is mindset and this is under your control when you learn to tune in. We have strategies throughout the book to help you do this.

Your Personal Dashboard: Measure Your Capacity

Self-awareness starts in your body. Part of your brain, called the insula, has a map of every organ in the body. This is how, what is happening in your body, is conveyed to the brain. This part of the brain is highly networked and when one of your emotions is triggered, your brain knows this is important.[4] This triggers the executive function of your brain to make a decision about how to react.

Distraction, increased pressure, the stress reaction unhooks the executive function, it goes offline, and your best behavior is hi-jacked. It pays to be aware of what is happening in your body. Learning to tune into your body will help you develop self-awareness, especially of your emotions. (In Chapter 7, you will read about the Body Scan, a great technique to check in and increase awareness.)

One way to learn what your body is telling you is with a personal dashboard. Create a two-column list, on one column list those indicators that drain your energy and take you off course, and in the next column, write out those indicators when you are optimized and performing at your best.

This includes everything from your energy, aches, tension, fatigue, attitude, to your overall lifestyle choices. These are all indicators of what may be going on within you. Keeping this type of dashboard increases your awareness.

Check out the sample dashboard of your personal capacity.

Personal Indicators	Warning Lights
Attitude of gratitude	Attitude is cynical, passive
Ability to smile, laugh	Increased drinking, fast food
Consistency in habits/ behaviors	Spending $$$$
Ability to focus	Irritability, fights, tension
Relaxed neck, back, shoulders	Tension, tightness, heartburn, headaches, etc.

Your capacity drives your performance and your ability to enjoy your life.

Your capacity is tied to performance and outcomes. It is the wild card that puts you ahead of the competition. Burning the candle at both ends, burns out the candle and you.

Think of a time you did not get the right amount of sleep or may have overindulged in some way the night before. What was the impact on your ability to be at the top of your game? How do you perform without enough sleep, when you are worried about your family, when you overindulge in food, or when you have conflicts in your significant relationships?

Which indicators increase your capacity? What lets you know you are performing optimally? Just like the dashboard on your car, what are your personal indicators that support performance? What are the warning lights?

Create your own dashboard with those indicators to monitor your ability to show up at your best. Later you can build on your new habit of awareness and tie these indicators to activities, habits and mindset. (Chapter 5 addresses Habits.)

What holds you back from being more aware?

Later in the book I talk about, not having enough time, too much to do, along with other distractions. We do provide strategies to help you deal with these. Keep in mind, these are not excuses to ignore what is happening in you. In fact, all of these are reasons to develop awareness quickly! They will de-rail and block your success.

Self-awareness only takes seconds once you learn to manage your attention. I will be discussing your attention and mindfulness in more detail in Chapters 2 and 8.

Increasing self-awareness begins with a decision, and then requires simple adjustments to monitor what is going on throughout your day.

I have included a variety of techniques in Chapter 8 to help you develop resilient thinking. We also have an online portal where you can access instructions on these techniques. Check out the Appendix for details on the Resilient Leader Toolkit.

Mindset Shift #2: How You Think (Anticipate)

When chronic stress or unchecked pressure takes over the higher functions of your brain, you lose a broad perspective; critical thinking is lost in the reactive nature of emotions.

As a leader being able to anticipate what may come up is important. Too often, the negative form of anticipation is activated; worry and rumination is what happens when the stress reaction is triggered. The brain is more negative when distracted and when the stress reaction is triggered.

Your brain does not know the difference between real or imagined scenarios, so if you tend to ruminate, you anticipate the worst-case scenario and block your ability to see potential.

Most of the time when taking a trip you get a map to show you the path forward. Leading a change initiative is no different. It is helpful to have a map of where you are going with milestones along the way to keep you on track. Do you have a map of what you want your operation to look like when it is finished? Have you done a value stream map of what your current state looks like? (Value stream mapping is a lean management approach to identify your current state. You can also use this to anticipate your future state, where you want to go.)

Create a map outlining all the changes required by various individuals as a result of your project. Visually depict what is happening, and what is expected to change. Identify the resistance, bottlenecks, and where you may have teams on board. Map out your communication strategies, in anticipation of what will be happening.

Having this map, you will avoid the blind spots created when distraction and stress short circuit your perspective.

You cannot anticipate without information. Do you know your people and how they might respond to the changes? Do you know their workload, and how it will be disrupted, as a result of the change?

Assumptions & Blind Spots

The ability to anticipate requires you know what is happening; you need relevant and current information. Too often, leaders do not have enough of the right information, and they operate off of assumptions that create blind spots. One assumption is that everyone knows their main goals and the purpose behind it.

A Harvard Business Review study reported ninety five percent of employees do not know the company's objectives, and how their job contributes to those objectives.[5] Recognizing major gaps in understanding, like this one, will help you take action. Chapter 6 discusses doing a Job Analysis with your team to bring everyone into alignment.

Are you making assumptions that blocks your ability to anticipate opportunities for improvement?

How you think (anticipate) means you engage with your future and identify value, respond to stakeholder needs, act on employee feedback, versus looking through the rear-view mirror and fixing problems.

Using a standardized problem-solving approach, without cutting corners, will help you anticipate and avoid blind spots. The lean sigma approach, DMAIC: define, measure, analyze, improve, control, increases the likelihood you will have the right information, focus on the right problem and find an ideal solution.

This sets up a continuous feedback loop, so you and the team learn from the process. It will help you avoid a common problem; the urge to jump to solutions before the problem is defined or well understood. This creates 'initiative mania' with too many priorities. This contributes to the change fatigue that is typical today.

Black and White Thinking (More Blind Spots)

"Are you with me, or not?" I heard my boss bark at me from his office. What a bind! If I disagreed with him about how to roll out this new product, he would see me as opposing him. And if I agreed with him, I would compromise myself because when it failed, I would be blamed.

Working in a black-and-white culture stymies growth; too much agreement is just as damaging as too much conflict.

Black-and-white thinking acts as a defense mechanism against uncertainty. Sometimes, people use it as a cover for always thinking they're right. I go into detail about bias and mindset distortions in Chapter 4.

Leaders get ahead because they are right! And the higher up you go, the more you'll tend to believe you're right. This can create a blind spot when leaders hire people who are more like them than different, creating an echo chamber.

Remember Melanie from the beginning of the chapter? She hired and fired a director in a 90-day period. You could almost get whiplash from the speed of that interaction. Her managers parroted her same talking points, since they learned early on that this was the way to get along with her.

Keep in mind, just because something feels right doesn't mean it is. The feeling of being right is not the result of critical reasoning; it comes from your emotional center. Melanie's blind spot was her feeling about the new director; it was rooted in bias, rather than an analysis of what the department needed.

Do you have people around you who ask questions and explore alternative scenarios, challenging the status quo? Or do you only surround yourself with people who agree with you?

It's normal for leaders to feel like they're right, and that can be a double-edged sword. When you never challenge this limited way of thinking, it becomes a blind spot.

One way to approach this conundrum is to develop your mindfulness. In Chapter 2, I talk about the power of the moment, the three seconds that offer you an opportunity to pause. Mindfulness means controlling your attention and being aware of what is happening within you—or around you—without judgement. The easier it is to control your attention and use the three seconds available in the moment, the more you'll learn.

This insight can undo a blind spot or a bias because you are refreshing your attention with new, timely, and relevant observations. Being able to master your attention is your most important skill.

To keep from getting stuck in your thinking, engage mindful attention practice. Mindful attention is a discipline of deliberately focusing your mind. It does not mean moving or thinking slowly, meditating on a cushion, chanting, or closing your eyes. It is a practice that increases your awareness, strengthens your presence, and reduces the chaos in your thinking under the stress reaction. Mindful attention is a choice between distraction (including internal ones) and being present in the moment.

There is more on mindful attention in Chapter 8.

The Number 1 Barrier to Future Success

A major blind spot most people do not recognize is the power of the past. Your past is the biggest barrier to future success. This is true even when the past has been successful—maybe even more true.

Have you ever thought to yourself? *I will never be able to do that again.* You end up settling for less believing you cannot recreate that level of success; you may underperform and do not fully commit to the effort. This blinds you to new and different approaches to the presenting challenge.

If you allow your self-belief, or your expectations to be trapped by what has happened in the past, whether successful or not, you cannot develop your potential or that of your team. We are hardwired to take what we learn from the past and project it into the future. Because our brain likes to conserve energy, it will fill in any gaps with assumptions and distorted thinking, unless you stay open by continually learning from your world around you.

This brings us to the third mindset shift, *what you do.*

Mindset Shift #3: What You Do (Agile)

Agile is a methodology, primarily used in the software world, to manage projects. It is based on iterative changes guiding the process, enabling the team to make rapid change based on feedback. It understands uncertainty is part of rapid change and provides an operational framework for the team to use.

Agile was "created" when a small group of developers decided they wanted to address what they were seeing in the workplace; stressed and pressured staff, missed deadlines and stalled projects. Organizations needed to be more responsive to customers, flexible and innovative. This was incompatible with top down leadership hierarchy. Agile has gone through its own evolution, and today the intention of agile is to delight customers, make the complex manageable, transform the organization's mindset and nurture the culture so everyone has the ability to do their best work.

Agile represents a mindset shift from top down planning and control to a cross functional team-based approach where you continually learn from mistakes, making it easier to embrace uncertainty and nurture innovation. This shift will increase your effectiveness and your impact as a leader.

Agile transformation is designed to manage accelerated change and prepare you to lead your followers through transition.

How do you become an agile thinker if you are not in any formal agile transformation? Adopting mindset one and two, *How You Feel* (Awareness) and *How You Think* (Anticipate), will help you engage an agile mindset, *What You Do*.

Let's look at an example.: an executive wants to set up a new department to handle the reorganization of his section. This has been suggested as the best practice for the industry. He decides to move ahead in creating this department and hires consultants to help him assess readiness and plan for what is needed. He needs to change how the current teams operate. However, he does not take the consultants' suggestion, or do his own assessment.

A year later, he has hired and fired more consultants, and progress is very slow. Fearing for his job, he is now micromanaging, increasing everyone's tension at work. Instead of working to improve, everyone is working to keep their jobs. Staff are now shackled to the status quo for fear of doing something that will anger their boss and get them fired.

An agile mindset recognizes the importance of first defining your desired outcomes. While best practices are good guidelines, they are not fixed rules. First, the leader with an agile mindset should increase their awareness of what the change will mean for their team—how does it impact their roles, their responsibilities, and how they feel about their work. This includes being aware of how the change will impact themselves as well as their team. Most leaders ignore the impact of the change on themselves.

In another example, this leader knows the move will generate a big change and decides to start with one team and use this team as a pilot. She carefully chooses a team with the skills to handle change, the ability to give feedback and the stamina to stick to the goals.

Once the team has developed the necessary skills to collaborate and function independently, this leader can then work with additional teams. Since the pilot team is further along and able to learn from their mistakes, they can share suggestions on how each subsequent team can improve the roll-out of their restructuring plan.

Using incremental change and learning from small "failures" enabled this leader and her teams to find what works best. This plan did not produce the widespread disruption and the ripples of fear, worry, and resistance that stalled progress in the previous department's example. The transformation of the department produced a continuous learning culture, which enabled everyone to better handle the ongoing demands for more change and increased value.

These examples are real world examples; both in the same company.

The leader who was successful in rolling out the changes initially looked like they were behind because she did not have the numbers to match the C-suite goals. Yet, because they did not have the fallout as in the other scenario, they quickly surpassed their goal and were able to exceed expectations.

The leader with the successful change made frequent revisions based on what was happening with the team, and not based on best practice, someone's opinion, or a previously defined plan that was not relevant to those currently doing the work.

Being agile in action means you use feedback and make incremental changes as needed vs being reactive to people and situations.

Chapter Overview

The premise of this book is to open your perspective and encourage you to evaluate your own mindset. Is it obstructing your success? I've arranged each chapter with questions, reflection exercises, and a summary at the end. I included study group exercises, making this a great book for your team to use as part of ongoing development.

This book offers a roadmap to tackle those elephants and makeover your mindset:

- **Chapter 2** begins with a three-step approach to focus on what is most important.

- **Chapter 3** looks at resilience and how to increase your capacity to perform. You also can take the assessment based on the Resilience Pyramid and find out what level of resilience needs more attention.

- **Chapter 4** explores the mindset distortions that may contribute to stalled progress, conflict and misunderstanding, limiting your ability to know what is really going on.

- **Chapter 5** breaks down the anatomy of a habit, giving you an easy way to interrupt habits that no longer work for you and build new ones.

- **Chapter 6** looks at why it can be so hard to get anything done at work. This chapter touches on important concepts like limiting work-in-progress and establishing priorities.

- **Chapter 7** introduces emotional intelligence and why this is one of the most distinguishing factors among successful leaders.

- **Chapter 8** introduces proven techniques and strategies you can use—right now—to transform the stress reaction.

- **Chapter 9** wraps up the book.

I have included tools and tips that can have an immediate impact on how you show up, your impact and presence. Take incremental steps toward the changes you seek and make small shifts in how you think.

Chapter Summary: The Elephant in the Room

- » The longer you avoid the difficult issues the heavier and tougher they get.

- » Elephants include:
    - o Stressed out staff
    - o Conflicts you ignore
    - o Lack of flexibility
    - o Resistance
    - o Status quo thinking

- » There is a revolving door with turnover and retention plaguing progress in most organizations.

- » Work is not working and there needs to be a new way to lead.

- » Your mindset is under your control. Learn to use it deliberately.

- » Three Mindset Makeovers:
    - o Self-awareness (Feel)
    - o Ability to anticipate (Think)
    - o Agile in action (Do)

Study Group Activity

» Identify the team's blind spots. Are there problems that you keep avoiding? Explore those problems that keep showing up.

» What mindset makeovers will make the biggest difference in your team, right now?

» How might your team make this shift?

For I know the plans I have for you, declares the LORD, plans to prosper you and not to harm you, to give you a future and a hope.

- Jeremiah 29:11

Chapter 3
Beyond Self-Doubt and Bias: Mindset Distortions

Successful people leverage their personalities to enhance their appeal, influence, and presence. The confidence necessary to do this has to be built on an authentic acceptance of one's strengths and potential. A healthy self-regard is one of the core elements of emotional intelligence.

I mention this because I see an epidemic of self-doubt, especially in women leaders. This is one of the biggest barriers to being effective and being taken seriously. Unchecked, I see it doing tremendous damage to the individual and instigating chaos and havoc in the workplace.

Because of this self-doubt, women end up making much less—as much as $20,000 less—than their male counterparts. This is definitely one of the elephants that, when ignored, gets bigger and heavier and more difficult to face.

In this chapter, I will talk about this and other mindset distortions because your mindset determines the actions you take and the decisions you make. Knowing how your mind works will help you transform this self-doubt and avoid biases that distort your perspective.

Self-doubt (and the fears that go along with it) can definitely be eliminated if you face it and acknowledge it's there. It is amazing how many leaders end up denying their self-doubt because its existence does not fit their view of how they are supposed to show up. I talk about the fatal emotion of denial in Chapter 7.

Self-doubt is usually more typical of women than men. However, as the pace of change accelerates and the landscape of roles and responsibilities change, both men and women are experiencing self-doubt as they wonder where they fit in this changing workplace. Men happen to have a built-in defense against self-doubt: they do not usually overthink how they show up. This is one time when women would benefit from being more like a man.

Self-doubt can be defined as uncertainty about one's basic worth and place in the world. It includes being worried if one's feelings are "legitimate;" taking responsibility for things that go wrong, whether or not you actually contributed to them; and being stuck in chronic self-consciousness. The dilemma of self-doubt is not limited to those who feel inferior to others— one can also feel superior to most everyone while also comparing themselves to others, just for different reasons. Self-doubt may or may not come with an avoidance of being in the spotlight.

Those who struggle with self-doubt have unrealistic expectations of relationships and often put intense pressure on the people around them. Part of this stems from needing validation and approval in order to feel good enough.

To make this even more confusing, self-doubt can be mixed with an overdose of confidence to disguise one's inner feelings of insecurity. In this case, perfectionism becomes the defense against feeling insecure, which sets up a vicious cycle. A new internal challenge emerges: perform perfectly, or face the self-doubt and feel the insecurity. Meanwhile, self-doubt in itself usually interferes with performance, leaving a residue of never being or doing enough.

If this is you or you know someone who fits this description, there is a way through this. First, acknowledge it. Let's talk a little more about this silent epidemic, and then we will get to the fears that can feed this dilemma.

Perfectionism

"Do as I say, not as I do." Did you get this message growing up? This is where this mindset distortion starts. Recently, I worked with a very successful business owner who achieved a great deal of success and notoriety, continuing into her late sixties. She came to me because she wanted to define her superpower and reset her brand to match her new goals.

She shared that despite her success, she always felt she had to do more than anyone else. This pressure to perform took all of her extra energy and kept her from investing in deep, personal relationships. She married late in life and confessed that she struggles making time for her husband, despite his interest in spending time with her. She was ready to confront this elephant because she could see what it was costing her. She wanted to have a more personable and authentic brand, and this required her to face her long-standing perfectionism and feelings of self-doubt.

I could relate as she spoke about the challenge of not knowing how much is enough. I am a "recovering" perfectionist, having once taken this to an art form. I know the struggle of wanting to be the best I can be and not knowing when enough is enough. I have learned this depends on the situation, the context of what is happening, and how much energy you have to invest at that particular moment.

There is no science to figuring this out; it requires taking a risk and increasing one's awareness. This will help you tell how much pressure you are putting on others because of your own self-doubt.

Developing healthy self-regard will not result in an absence of any of these fears and bias, but it will help you recognize they are there and then adjust for them. This is how the three mindset shifts come together: awareness, anticipation, and agility. You will be aware and acknowledge the perfectionism (self-doubt); anticipate when it shows up in high-pressure situations; and then be flexible and emotionally agile, shifting out of your default mode.

Here is an example: let's say overthinking, also known as worry and rumination, is your default reaction to feeling pressured. This is a trigger to overdo out of fear. Instead, you can anticipate this and set up another action, like checking in with a trusted colleague and getting a reality check about how much is enough.

In this situation, executive coaching can have a profound impact on your old, outdated mindset distortion and help you build up a healthy and powerful self-regard.

I talk more about confidence and confidence killers in Chapter 7 on emotional intelligence. Let's talk now about fears that can derail your influence and impact.

Fear of Criticism

You must develop a thick skin. Criticism goes with the job. When you are out in front, you will be held responsible for what happens. Sometimes the criticism is justified and other times you are just the target for other people's frustrations.

Get out in front of it; increase your awareness. Ask your team, "How am I doing? What else can I do to help you do your job better?"

These questions demonstrate you are interested and concerned about your team. From their answers you will learn their perspective and how you are impacting others. This builds respect; humility goes a long way to building trust.

Fear of Inadequacy

Confidence is a skill set that is strengthened in the line of fire. Taking risks, trying new behaviors, and going beyond your comfort zone builds confidence. This fear of inadequacy will hold you back. This is an old fear that can get tripped with uncertainty, new experiences, and a lack of awareness.

When this fear of inadequacy is tripped, most people compare how they feel on the inside with how others appear on the outside and most always find themselves lacking.

Resist comparing yourself to <u>anyone</u>. Recognize you are unique and have a set of skills and expertise all your own. Own it.

When you embrace those areas, you know you need to work on, this fear shrinks. Taking charge of your development is powerful.

Being willing to learn and grow is one of the dimensions in emotional intelligence that will take you a long way on the path to leadership success.

Use the Incremental Change Worksheet in the Appendix and keep track of those skills you need and what you want to learn. Use the Action Plan next to it, to take you through the next year to acquire those skills.

Fear of Failure

No one likes the feeling of failure, especially high achievers, and leaders. Just like criticism, failure is part of the territory as a leader. Whether it comes in the form of missed deadlines, decisions that cost money, bad hires, or failing to act, it is learning from these mistakes that really matters. What is problematic is when you keep doing what you have always done, and nothing changes.

Learning from your mistakes is when you review what happened and ask, "how could I have done this differently?" Then you take action.

Fear of failure can turn into rumination about failing. Have you stayed up all night thinking about all those things that could go wrong? Maybe you have taken on a new role and you worry, thinking about the guy who was fired before you, or when you let the two fears just mentioned take over your mindset, and you lose confidence. Then failure becomes a self-fulfilling prophecy. Ruminating is not a strategy; it is a defense against uncertainty.

Make the uncertain more certain with a plan.

There are exercises throughout this book, especially in Chapter 8, on how to unhook from the narrow perspective of the stress reaction. As you grow in awareness and build your confidence, these fears will lessen.

Fear of Making Critical Decisions

Some decisions need to be made quickly; others need to go through some analysis. Refusing to make the decision and taking the "wait and see" attitude or being stuck in analysis paralysis is not good for your credibility as a leader.

Develop systems to help you get the needed information, identify risks and evaluate consequences then decide. Review the impact of the decision to learn from it, deciding what, if anything, needs to change. Then move on.

Having these fears is not the problem. It is when you choose to deny them, pretend they will go away on their own, or you can 'fake it till you make it.' Denial doesn't let you prepare or develop new skills.

Deal with the fears or they deal with you. This is the value of coaching. Talking confidentially with a professional coach helps you *quickly* move through the fears and learn what you need to learn.

Bias: Mindset Distortion

Most of us think of ourselves as rational and capable of making good decisions. Yet the difference between a good decision and one that isn't could be a bias. Bias in our thinking (cognitive distortions) are inherent in everyone's thinking. These distortions impact our decisions in subtle ways.

The bias may show up skewing your thinking to be more optimistic, negative, rigid, self-centered, among others, causing you to over or underestimate the project, your ability or someone else's' ability. Either way, thinking becomes more reactive in the presence of bias.

Remember that ninety percent of what happens during the day is driven through the automatic mind, your unconscious mind. Your brain will fill in gaps in perception to be efficient and save energy.

Magicians use the brain's natural processing to create the illusion we call magic. By directing your conscious mind, "look over here at this card and only this card," your attention is manipulated, and your working memory is overloaded. This is how distraction works, increasing the risk of mindset distortions.

The workday rarely has time built in to think; this increases the risk of mindset distortions.

How often do you evaluate whether your decisions are good and bias free?

There are over one hundred biases listed in Wikipedia. This is over one hundred ways we can distort information. Through observation or interaction, we take information in, process it through our filters, which includes fears and bias, both falling under the radar of consciousness. As you make decisions (or choose not to make the decision) how do you know you are not distorting information with an expectation bias, or a distortion bias, or a status quo bias, and the list goes on?

Bias will steer our thoughts and decisions in subtle ways, we may end up being more optimistic than realistic, fall prey to a confirmation bias, or get caught up in a fear scenario that has little probability of happening but feels scary.

Here are a few biases to be aware of:

Blind spot bias

This is when you deny your own biases. In other words, everyone else is biased and I am not. I am too intelligent, smart, savvy, you name it. The truth is, we are all potentially guilty of all these biases. Acknowledgement is the first step to overcoming them. Use a mindfulness practice to expand your awareness and avoid reaction out of the limited perspective of the stress reaction.

Confirmation bias

This is what leads you to look for evidence to support what you already know. You view the facts as either confirmation of what you know, or you discount any facts that do not support your view. When you find yourself "shopping" for the option that matches what you want, you are under the influence of the confirmation bias.

Anchoring effect

This is the tendency to rely on the initial piece of evidence you encounter. This is what happens in negotiation, the initial number presented, anchors in the bidding going forward.

It is helpful to review the evidence, pros and con, when making a decision, and potentially avoiding this bias.

Optimism bias

This leads one to underestimate projects, overlooking potential pitfalls, ignoring all the costs and duration of the project.

An optimism bias is different from being optimistic. Bias is a blind spot. The highest and best expression of optimism means you are also realistic.

Availability bias

This mindset distortion is when we rely on those things that come to mind quickly as more representative than they really are. This reliance on things that come to mind quickly gives us the illusion we are making solid quick decisions and judgments. This bias avoids time-consuming fact checking and research which can be convenient when you want a quick decision, but the decision will lack an adequate vetting.

Estimation bias (fundamental attribution error)

This is when you overestimate someone's weakness (internal characteristics) and underestimate circumstances. *Have you ever judged someone for not having any willpower and then had to explain why you are going back for seconds on your diet?*

The tendency is to also underestimate the influence of our choices and overestimate circumstances.

Example: This is when you blame outside circumstances for why things did not get done, even though you did not spend the time needed on the project.

This bias happens frequently and is the source of conflict and misunderstanding. Too often, we routinely ignore situational influences and rush to judgement about someone. This is when you blame someone for what happened despite circumstances.

For example, have you accused a coworker of being lazy and this is why you missed the deadline, when the office was closed for 3 days due to unusual weather? Consider giving people the benefit of the doubt to avoid attributing negative judgements.

When you are peeved by someone's behavior, identify 2-4 positive attributes in that individual. It will balance your opinion.

This may help you see if this is a projection of your own unidentified behavior.

Research has found that because of the unconscious influence of emotions and the amount of information the unconscious takes in compared to the conscious mind, "reality" is not perceived directly.

Much of what you "know" and even observe is filtered through the lens of your early experiences and your belief systems. The mind filters everything that happens to us through this lens of our internal mental models and these biases.

How can you improve your thinking?

First realize there is a lot more going in internally than we realize. Reducing pressure and stress allows one to access higher functions of the brain, broaden perspective and decrease reactions. Under stress the brain is hardwired to survive, and distortions are common under these conditions.

It takes a deliberate effort and self-regulation to engage your brain's highest functions. This is thriving, not just surviving.

Managing emotions and regulating one's internal impulses will improve your thinking. Without the emotional reactions, you can thoughtfully consider what is happening and evaluate the context, versus rushing to judgement.

Self-awareness and self-regulation are the foundation of emotional intelligence.

Tips to power up your thinking:

1. Use reflection to evaluate your thinking and your decisions.

2. Begin a mindfulness practice to slow down chaotic thinking and expand your observation.

3. Engage in a systematic problem-solving approach like lean sigma. Use this approach without compromise and you will avoid distortions.

4. Consider others may be right more often that you think!

Chapter Summary: Beyond Fear and Bias

- » We all have fears. But when these fears are outside your everyday awareness, they will sabotage you.

- » Fears of criticism, failure, and inadequacy can paralyze you. ***Super tip: Stop comparing yourself to other people.***

- » Bias is a natural tendency *we all have*. Learn to evaluate your decisions and your observations to improve your thinking.

- » There is a tendency to overestimate one's strengths. Engage in a professional development plan.

- » Status quo is the resistance that stalls innovation and creativity.

- » Keep an idea journal, and record thoughts and ideas.

- » Play more.

Study Group Activity

- » Discuss how the group can avoid biases.

- » Engage in communication and collaboration skills training. Group members need to learn how to present their arguments and listen to opposing viewpoints.

- » Ask each member to share their biggest fear.

- » Explore how members of the group can help each other.

Chapter 4
Habits: For Better or Worse

Think about your day. What do you when you wake up? If you run, how do you tie your shoes? What are the habits that drive you? Researchers say 40% (and maybe more) of what you do during the day is a habit. And 90% of what we do is directed by our unconscious mind and happens automatically.

What this means is that you are forming habits without even realizing it.

Driving to work, you automatically turn the wheel, turn on the blinker, and handle the car, without having to think about it. This saves energy; it is your brain being efficient. You may also be stopping in the cafeteria and picking up a brownie, automatically, because it picks you up in the late morning. This is a new habit you have developed, without realizing it.

In this section, we are going to explore how habits are formed and how to change habits that get in the way of you being your best.

Our nervous system, especially our brain, loves two things - to keep us safe and conserve energy. Habits are how our nervous system functions. For now, rather than thinking of habits as good or bad, look at habits as ways of simplifying how you get things done. Imagine if you had to think about every activity in your day from scratch? You would be exhausted by 9 a.m.

Brushing your teeth, making coffee, lacing up your running shoes, and so many other habits help you throughout your day. These habits were started because they initially helped you achieve a goal. And there are other habits that may have started in the fog of distraction and are now interfering with your daily performance.

Many habits aren't even labeled as "bad" by most people but can be interfering with you being your best. Could your habit of complaining when you are given a new assignment be the reason your boss overlooked you for the promotion? Complaining slows your progress, interferes with your internal creativity, and leaves your boss with the wrong impression. Yet, you may not notice it or realize it's a habit.

Are you interacting with your team members in a habitual way? Does it feel wooden or animated? Try asking more questions and spend time simply listening.

To identify your habits, think about any outcomes you do not regularly achieve. Then, walk back and look closely at your routines or thought processes related to that outcome. Ask yourself, does this habit advance my progress or keep me going in circles?

Which habits do you want to change because they are interfering with making progress?

Take a deep breath and think through your day, from the time you get up in the morning to the time you go to bed. Draw a timeline of your habits. Which habits create a chain reaction that may be sabotaging your best later in the day?

Let's say you drink a lot of coffee and want to cut back because it makes you tense at work. When you look at your entire day, you realize that you unwind at night by scrolling through social media, which keeps you up later at night than you would like. You are tired when you wake up and use coffee to get you going in the morning. The habit to change first, might be staying up late, and scrolling through social media.

Increasing your awareness of what you are doing and why, will serve you with any habit, you want to break and then rebuild. Once you understand what happens in a habit—its structure—you can make those incremental changes that add up to big changes.

Increasing your awareness and mindful attention is especially helpful; most of your daily activity is driven by your automatic mind, your unconscious.

For example, imagine walking to a meeting. You skipped lunch and are hungry, the reports came back with less than stellar numbers, you are disappointed, you remember how your boss reacted the last time this happened, and the noise coming from the construction outside is louder than you recall. As you leave the meeting, you have an urge for chocolate, even though you know it makes you sleepy. You rush to the cafeteria and quickly down a piece of cake. You are sluggish and trouble focusing at your next meeting. You were so distracted by the overload of stimuli that you did not stop to consider the consequences of that decision.

Your automatic mind was in charge, making associations as you walked down the hall, distracted by this internal noise. This decision may not seem that bad, but there are other choices one makes that can have much more serious consequences.

The more aware you are, of your associations, the easier it is to tease out the cues for your habits.

Reboot your attention, be in the moment, whether you are at work or at home or out socially. This awareness becomes part of your natural mindful attention when you commit to building this productive habit.

Habits form because the brain wants to save energy; its instinct is to turn everything into a habit. But because survival is paramount to the primitive brain, it recognizes that it cannot lose attention and miss something that may threaten it. To manage this initial uncertainty, the brain will establish a cue that lets it know which pattern to use.

In my private practice, I used hypnotherapy to help smokers quit. When identifying cravings, a very difficult craving to stop was smoking in the car. The cue was putting the key in the ignition: that told their brain it was time to light up. The cue for any craving alerts your nervous system for a specific routine and reward loop. The reward tells your brain to remember this routine.

The structure of a habit is the cue, routine, and reward.

The more you engage in this habit, the more automatic it becomes, until you begin to anticipate and crave the reward. To change the habit, you want to change the routine—the response to the cue.

You also want to understand what the cue is and why it is necessary. Let's go back to the example of complaining every time you are given a new assignment. The cue is the anxiety you feel when your boss gives you something new to do. When you slow everything down, you recognize the thoughts running through your mind: "Do I have the time?" "Can I do this?" This created anxiety and the complaining reduces the anxiety you felt, which is the reward.

To change the habit, change the routine.

Instead of complaining, which interferes with your performance and gives your boss the wrong impression about you, you can ask questions about what the assignment entails. This will give you the same reward—relief from anxiety—but ultimately better outcomes.

This change in habit also helps you feel better about yourself, puts you in a learning mode on the job, and will open opportunity as people around you see a shift in attitude.

What mental or emotional habits are obstructing your success?

Take this as a challenge to shift out of autopilot—going through the motions and engaging in old and familiar routines because your brain wants to be safe and efficient—and shift into living a no-excuses life.

Infrastructure Habits (The Habits to Build On)

You know now that most of your day-to-day activity is designed around habits—some good and others not so much. And you have probably tried to change your habits many different times. Did you know that certain habits provide a structure for other habits to thrive—or not?

Think about your day: what habits give you the most energy and vitality to perform at your best?

Discover when you are at your best, early morning, mid-morning, etc. Do you most creative work then.

For most people, sleep habits, diet, drinking enough water to energize you, exercise, and some type of prayer, meditation, or stress relief are the "Infrastructure Habits" that help you build on other great habits. This also supports a power mindset.

Consider this: when you are well rested, you wake up earlier, have more time in your day, are more energized, and are probably happier. This builds your confidence and feeds the desire to keep your momentum going.

What happens when you do not sleep well? You compensate for the lack of energy and focus and may use caffeine to overstimulate, which has consequences, like increased irritability and sleep interference. The vicious cycle is born.

Download the Habit Tracker worksheet to track your habits. (Access in online membership). It includes space for you to write in those habits that keep you well fueled and focused.

The main goal of these exercises is to increase your awareness. Learn more about yourself—what increases your motivation and what decreases it.

There are days when the loss of motivation is subtle, and without the habit of reflection, you will miss the trigger that derails you. (Use the Daily Review described in the online course.)

Infrastructure Habits Include:

- Sleep habits
- Food/fuel (what type of food plan best serves your energy?)
- Water/hydration
- Exercise/movement
- Inspiration/spiritual food
- Financial/savings goals

Evaluate your day and see how well you are tuned in to these basic habits. Use your Habit Tracker to monitor these habits. You may find that stabilizing these habits will help you make changes in other areas easier.

I have seen the desire for destructive habits disappear once you stabilize these foundational habits. The cue can disappear for those unhealthy or unproductive habits that are compensating for one of the infrastructure habits that's lacking.

This brings us to the mindset habits that are foundational to living a no-excuses life.

Mindset Habits

Henry Ford said it best: "Whether you think you can, or you think you can't, you are right."

Mindset is everything. If you do not believe you can do something, you are not going to try. This is true in relationships as well as at work. Research has found that when one partner puts demands on the other, if that partner does not feel they can meet those demands, they don't even try.

Think about your own life. Is there an area you would like to improve, but your mindset is negative? How is this impacting your progress?

Check out these mindset habits that build consistent success:

Optimism

Yes, I've mentioned the Optimism Bias. However, being optimistic is different. It means, you recognize your strengths and keep going, despite the challenge in front of you. It takes into account the reality on the ground, the context of what is happening and does not over or underestimate this.

Being optimistic includes confidence in your ability to meet challenges.

Coachability (Action)

This is your willingness to learn times your willingness to act. Research shows those who act within 24 hours end up achieving more.

Flexibility

Change is the new normal; the rate and pace of change today is unprecedented. When you adopt a continual learning mindset, you are able to quickly reevaluate your options, and are open to change. This is a win-win. The person with the greatest flexibility in their behavior controls the outcome in relationships or negotiation.

Focus

Your attention is your greatest asset. Distractions drain your energy and destroy the ability to finish tasks and do a job well. Having a focused mindset helps you concentrate and prioritize the most important tasks.

These mindset habits will make it easier to develop new high-performance habits.

From Autopilot to Power Mindset

Your primitive brain is like the thermostat in your home. Once you set it at a certain temperature, it turns the system on and off to keep the temperature stable. Unfortunately, this safe and efficient system will not produce peak performance, innovation, or inspiration. Its job is to keep you safe and to conserve energy. It is up to you to power up your brain and go beyond the autopilot settings.

Consider the tools you are learning in this program as your upgrade for your thinking.

Your brain is an amazing structure: 86 billion neurons, communicating with your entire body through synaptic connections and a host of biochemicals that travel throughout, creating sensations, emotions, and impressions and stimulating critical functions for your health and wellbeing. Through research on neuroplasticity, we now know that your brain is plastic. When given the opportunity, your brain learns and adapts. Your brain builds neural pathways and sets up default modes of responding.

Neuroplasticity demonstrates that the brain is capable of learning new ways of doing things—provided you try new ways to do things. If you always respond the way you have always responded, you will always react the way you have always reacted.

This routine sets up a default pathway in your brain, making it easier to respond that way all the time.

Do you frequently complain? Are you easily angered or feel resentful? Do you look for shortcuts, even when you know going through the process as expected will yield better results?

Habits of mind—as well as physical habits like smoking, drinking, or using substances to alter your mood—can all be changed by exploring your cues and changing your routines.

You can power up your mindset using these suggestions by increasing the following in your day:

1. **Gratitude** changes the way your brain works and stimulates a different set of hormones that broadens your perspective.

2. **Curiosity** increases the firing of different neurons. The brain loves novelty and will open new opportunity for your thought processes.

3. **Physical exercise** stimulates your thinking. In just 15 minutes per day, you can increase your productivity by over 25%.

You were born with an amazing brain. Unlock its powerhouse of resources with a resilient mindset.

Chapter Summary: Habits

- » Habits form more easily when you're distracted.
- » Infrastructure habits can make other habits easier to build.
- » Did you know that certain habits provide a structure for other habits to thrive—or not?
- » Recognize your habits. Monitor them for consistency. Use the Habit Tracker.
- » Habits have three parts: cue, routine, and reward. Identify the cue. Change the routine.
- » Build mindsets of optimism, coachability, flexibility and focus.
- » Be curious, grateful and exercise to power up your mindset.

Study Group Activity

» Does the group have habits that get in the way of being better?

» Identify them. What new habits are needed?

» Identify how you—as a group—will be consistent with the habits that increase performance.

Chapter 5
Why Can't I Get Anything Done at Work?

Mary Lou is committed to her job. She loves being the director of marketing and takes pride in her ability to manage the department. In the last year, there has been increased pressure to reduce costs and improve customer satisfaction scores. Mary Lou doesn't realize she has become tense and irritable with her team.

The account manager, Jason, meets with Mary Lou weekly, and he is on edge, just thinking about the meeting. Before he can even sit down, Mary Lou has attacked his decision on the timeline for rolling out the new plan. There is no discussion. He is thinking about leaving the position but keeps his plans to himself.

The wake-up call for May Lou comes when her long-time friend expresses concern about her level of tension and stress. Mary Lou decides she needs to do something different. She has been feeling guilty and pressured, and deep down she knows she has not been communicating effectively. Feeling the pressure to meet her goals, she has lost her perspective.

This is a typical scenario of how the stress reaction slowly erodes confidence and clarity in leaders. The more pressure one feels to perform, the harder it becomes to stay focused, emotionally flexible, and empathetic. The stress reaction blocks higher levels of problem solving and effective communication. Instead, there is the tendency to micromanage (over-control); communicate in short, terse commands, and view followers as incompetent.

The ability to solve problems is lost when working under the impact of a chronic stress reaction. With the higher functions of your cortex unavailable, and the reactive impulsive primitive part of the brain, in charge, you end up working harder, longer hours, without accomplishing your goals.

Distractions, delays, misunderstanding is filling the typical workday making it difficult to make progress.

This is the vicious cycle of distraction. Making progress is a major motivator for people and the chronic distraction dulls the momentum.

Does this sound like your typical day at work?

- » 2-3 hours, daily, on emails alone.
- » Every three minutes there is an interruption.
- » 50% of what is done is a do-over.
- » 70% of error is due to a communication breakdown.
- » Roughly $500 billion is lost because of workplace stress.
- » 70% of workers are on autopilot.

Did you know a 15 second distraction costs 20 minutes in concentration?

Common Energy Drains at Work

Work has become a major stressor for many people. Communication breakdown, conflict, initiative overload, bad bosses, complexity, and daily hassles interfere with getting the job done. [8]

When you can engage your resilient thinking, you learn to focus and get beyond the distractions, stress, and internal emotional distress that distorts your ability to communicate.

The brain has a mental default mode and will fill in words or solutions—even if they are not there—to fill a gap. Your mental default mode goes into gear when you are under stress or too much pressure. The longer you look at a problem, in the same way, the more likely you will get stuck using your mental default. If you are distracted and lack focus, your mental default may be how you go through your day.

This is limiting!

I have found that as distraction increases, so does the sense of urgency; it is this urgency that short circuits resilient thinking.

Talking with hundreds of professionals and leaders, I have heard them mention the following stressors and energy drains:

1. Never enough time
2. Too much to do & lack of priorities
3. Status quo
4. Office politics (drama)

We will go through each one in more detail, giving you practical ways to develop your resilient thinking.

There Is Never Enough Time

There will always be twenty-four hours in the day. Cutting back on sleep, self-care, family time, or time to plan, think, and create is not a long-term strategy to be more productive. In fact, the more you try to speed up to get more done, the more exhausted you'll feel and the less you'll accomplish.

Yes, it is true! Nowadays, we must do more with fewer resources in the course of a day. Most people believe that "smart" technology should make them more efficient, if not smarter. Right? Yet, technology has changed the way the brain works.

Research shows that younger people are more forgetful than older people when challenged to sustain attention and to think deeply.[9] The loss of reflection and contemplation has caused a decrease in the ability to solve problems and find innovative solutions.

Smart phones and the internet are often more of a distraction than a time saver. Unfortunately, having so much information readily available at your fingertips doesn't make anyone smarter. Studies reveal it decreases your ability to form memories of what you just learned. Increased distraction makes it harder for the brain to move this information from working memory to long-term memory, where this learning can be consolidated for later use.

Research shows half of what we get done during the day is a do-over. As forgetfulness increases, there may be even less time available.

How much time do you spend doing something over, restarting a project, or getting delayed by interruptions?

Do you have a strategy to manage interruptions? Or do you make yourself available at any time, thinking this will build trust with your followers? You may be short-changing your own performance by stretching yourself so thin that it makes it impossible to be present with the person in front of you.

As mentioned earlier, constant interruptions and the inability to concentrate increases the sense of urgency, compelling many leaders to spend their energy and internal resources on the *most urgent* issues that show up. This leaves the most important work sidelined *for when there is time to get to it*—which never seems to come. Sound familiar?

Please understand, I know there are time constraints with the amount of work that needs to be done and the deadlines and crises that arise. This makes the case even more urgent for focus. Eliminate interruptions and the sense of urgency that follows the interruptions. Since there will always be 24 hours in the day (and multitasking has proven counterproductive), **you need a plan to manage interruptions and focus.**

Unchecked stress threatens your ability to perform well—this is the nature of the stress reaction. Excess cortisol interrupts the prefrontal cortex, which is responsible for regulating and controlling your working memory. This compromises your ability to think through problems, make good judgments, be flexible, plan, and execute ideas. Aspects of strategic thinking—like being creative, empathetic, optimistic, and present—are shut down.

Taking time to think through your strategic goals and the progress you've (or haven't made) toward them is necessary for agility—and this is one of the first things to go when the sense of urgency kicks in. Resilient thinking is not usually a "skill set" on a performance review, and with the tsunami of interruptions, overwhelm, and urgency that drain valuable energy, leaders need to think strategically: perhaps resilient thinking *should* be considered.

Without the ability to manage one's own internal distractions and focus, results fall short, and perspectives shrink.

We talked about the "Daily Review" in Chapter 2 on Focus. Use this every day; it gives you data and information you need to make adjustments going forward.

Most Plans Fail - Why?

To make the most of your time, you need a plan. There are different ways to approach planning and making plans. We are going to briefly look at the most challenging aspect of planning: execution.

A strategic plan is a high-level overview, which projects long-term strategies and lays out *why* something needs to happen. While this high-level plan is essential, Churchill said it best: *Every now and then, you should look at the results.*

There are many planning processes that help leaders focus and leverage: OKRs, 4DX, and X Matrix, among others. Though amazing at helping you write the plan, they do not address how to get people to change their mindset and behavior and do something differently. This is the challenge of execution and the focus of this book: shifting mindset to increase capacity.

This is one of the elephants. Most plans fail to deliver. I believe it is because most leaders do not consider what it takes to change the behavior of their teams.

Strategic plans—and even operational plans—sound good on paper until you go deeper and look at what would be required to make the results happen. A question that needs to be considered is:

What percentage of people have to change what they do in a typical day to make the plan work?

Understanding the extent of change will help you plan your execution strategy.

It is frustrating (and can be draining) for leaders when the team isn't doing what needs to be done at the required level, and it seems logical to blame the team. Yet, if most of the team members are not following through, it is a problem in the system and not with the people.

As the leader, *you are accountable for the system*, making it even more tempting to blame the team—after all, it would work if they would just do their jobs!

But what *is* their job? Interestingly, workflow studies have shown that 85% of the employees surveyed did not understand the goal they were pursuing. They either could not name it, or the goal wasn't what they thought it was. The Job Analysis in the next section is a great strategy to counter this.

If it isn't the people, why do so many plans fail? What really gets in the way of executing the best-laid plans? It is what keeps many people busy during the day but keeping them from the important work.

"Work" can refer to the daily activities required to make the strategic goals a reality, as well as all the other activities competing for the same attention and commitment from the workforce. We talked early on about retention, engagement strategies, and employee stress taking up major resources. How do these issues impact employees' ability to focus on what is most important?

Do you often have urgent things pop up, distracting people from the critical mission at hand? Does the team know what the top priority is? Shortly, I'll go over the priority matrix, a tool to help define the jobs people have to do and sort them based on priority.

But, if there are too many priorities, there is too much work. I talk about limiting work in progress in the section on priorities.

Before we get there, consider your work situation. What is your reaction when there is a delay, or the team doesn't execute a plan correctly? Do you take on more responsibility, come in early and work when it is quiet to pick up the slack? How does this impact your ability to provide oversight? Does it cramp your leadership? What does it communicate to your team?

Successful execution requires a willingness to go beyond the status quo ("this is the way we have always done it") and the ability to focus and manage the many distractions that come up during the day.

To get results you have never gotten before; you have to do something you have never done.

Are you willing to change how you lead?

Why Goals Fail to Engage

Let's talk about this elephant in the room: getting people to do something differently in the face of unmet goals and failed plans. You are not alone. 90% of goals are left unaccomplished. This contributes to the failure of plans.

Goals become delayed or diluted and plans often get discarded because they seem too hard or impossible to execute.

Let's look at some of the reasons people fail to achieve their goals. This occurs even with the SMART goal process. (Specific, Measurable, Attainable, Relevant, Timely.)

The goals are vague.

Goals that are not measurable won't stick. If you don't know where the finish line is, you'll be less motivated to reach it. It's human nature: we only try when we're sure we can achieve what we set out to achieve.

Solution: Make your goals specific and measurable. What will you see that lets you know you have arrived at your goal?

Goals lack relevance and meaning.

Meaning and purpose are the top drivers of motivation. Knowing your "why" will keep you focused on the end result, even when you may have lost that lovin' feeling for your goal. After the honeymoon period wears off and you are faced with challenges related to achieving your goal, you need to have a strong "why" to keep from quitting.

Solution: Use the 5 Whys to get to the fundamental reason you are doing what you are doing. Not sure about the 5 Whys? Check the Appendix.

The nays have it.

Goals and plans can bring out the naysayers.

When constructing goals at work, engage the entire team in the process. This way they own it. Use the Five Why's to get to the fundamental motivation behind the goal. Evaluate everyone's commitment. What needs to happen to increase that commitment?

If these are personal goals, they are *yours*. They do not require consensus or approval. Even well-intentioned friends and family members can discourage you from going for it. Other people might be jealous and seek to hold you back, so you won't make them look bad.

Too many worthy goals are lost because friends, family, and naysayers end up influencing the level of commitment to the desired outcome.

Solution: Find your why (done in the previous step) and keep that in the front of your mind, or your team's mind. Work on your confidence and wean yourself from needing the approval of others. This makes the naysayers less persuasive.

Procrastination.

This shows up in different ways. Perfectionists struggle with putting things off because if it cannot be done perfectly, then they continue to "work on it" until they feel ready. Unfortunately, that time never comes.

Solution: The above suggestions will help with procrastination. If you do struggle with perfectionism, acknowledge, and work on that.

Too much to do (including distractions).

In the next section, I talk about priorities and limiting the amount of work in progress. This is an epidemic problem. "Being busy" is worn like a badge of honor, regardless of what actually gets accomplished.

Solution: Spend time deciding what you need to be busy doing.

Researchers have found that plans containing incremental goals are more motivating. People achieve these goals more quickly as opposed to a broadly stated long-term plan. This is due in part to the ability to connect the dots between the plan and the outcome. Making progress is one of the top motivators, so having smaller goals can be a key driver of performance.

The other factor is simple: shorter goals are more flexible and can be revised as needed. This flexibility is encouraging. Most people do not want to be locked into a plan that stops working. In fact, researchers have found that when plans conflict, rumination replaces creativity.

Suggestion: Set up 30-day plans with 10-day incremental steps. Watch what happens to your team's performance! This will require more planning time, so you should include your team in the planning process.

Too Much to Do and a Lack of Priorities

Do you have a plate full of emergencies? Is everything a priority? When you get overloaded during the day, it becomes impossible to know your priorities, and it is easy to get sidetracked by everyone else's issues.

Before we talk about priorities, this scenario is a symptom of a bigger problem: too much work in the queue. When it becomes difficult to establish priorities, that means you do not have a system in place to decide which projects get worked on and when.

As a lean sigma consultant, I have seen this scenario play out over and over. Without a problem-solving system, people tend to jump to solutions without defining the real problem. They end up with initiative overload and simply too much to do. It becomes hard to prioritize, especially when others are setting the priority.

I have an online course on problem solving at Work Smart Club. I highly recommend it. You can find more information in the Appendix. For now, you can implement the following tips.

It is necessary to be clear about your goals. What is most important for you at this time, and when does it have to get done? Here are some suggestions to help you prioritize.

Visualize Your Work

To help you understand workflow—what is being worked on and the bottlenecks that exist—I suggest Kanban boards to visualize the flow. This also allows you highlight strategic goals and see how the work flows, how to feed in new work as well as track communication throughout the process.

The brain processes visual information 60,000 times faster than text.[10] The brain naturally thinks in images; the retina is the connection for almost half of all nerve fibers coming into the brain.

Using colorful post-it notes on a whiteboard makes it very easy to see what work needs to be done, who is working on it, and what else is happening. Visualizing your team's workflow gives you (and everyone on the team) an immediate picture of workload.

You can hold "board meetings" right in front of the white boards and discuss what is happening and what is needed. These meetings are short, focused on bottlenecks and what needs to happen to resolve them, workload, who might be burdened, who can help, while documenting progress reports. The type and frequency of meetings is decided on during the planning stage of the project. Teams find it very effective to meet more often and in shorter increments to build follow-through and ownership of the tasks.

This is the first step to developing a system to keep the work flowing. You will want to establish a plan to deal with the backlog, bottlenecks, and emergencies. If you have department or organizational goals, include them on the board to help everyone make the connection between what they are doing and the overall organizational objective.

Limit Your Work in Progress (WIP)

"Work in progress" is a term used in supply chain management to indicate the partially unfinished work or the value of goods. Limiting WIP is used as part of the agile transformation in the software industry to improve productivity. I see a tremendous application for WIP limits in any workspace.

Think of WIP as the work you are currently doing. Whether you are looking at an individual or the entire department, there is a certain capacity one has—or the department has—to get things done. This book has been talking about exceeding one's internal capacity and the consequences of doing so; the same is true of workload. When you exceed the capacity of the department, you end up with workarounds, errors, costly mistakes, and burned-out staff.

When workflow is invisible, there are no widgets to count or obvious production cues. In healthcare, insurance, design, and other industries, adding new work does not have an obvious impact. Without any system in place to channel workflow, most people will work longer and harder to catch up, and we all know how that turns out.

You must have a system in place that deals with workflow.

When work is not limited, you end up with increased stress and initiative overload. Here is how it played out in one company. The top executives knew they needed to introduce more product into the marketplace to stay competitive. One of the VPs put together a small work team that worked off site and designed several new products in a short period of time. They were able to launch them quickly and had success in the market.

Another VP set up a "Department of Innovation & Creativity" and redesigned everyone's roles and titles. A year later, they are struggling to function as a team with little to show for their effort.

The second VP was unable to produce because he lacked clarity around his goals and threw too much at the team to do. These are typical barriers to productivity in the workplace and a source of stress.

How do you limit WIP?

You must first know what you want to get done. Having a clear goal is the most important part of top performance—even more important than having the right team, assets, or enough time.

The graphic on the next page outlines 5 Steps to optimize your workflow.

1. Begin where you are (vs looking at where you want to be after the change) and outline roles and responsibilities.

2. Visualize the work using a Kanban board.

3. Decide on how work gets done, making this clear & visual.

4. Measure and manage workflow. On the Kanban, set up a column for "Que," work that needs to be done in

the future as well as a backlog, work that is not able to be done now.

5. Set up communication loops using 5-minute stand up meetings around the Kanban board to discuss bottlenecks and challenges.

Optimize workflow—limit WIP.

This process is similar to value stream mapping; begin with mapping where you are and who does what. Until you thoroughly understand how workflows, and how decisions get made about what work gets done, you cannot make good decisions about to change the work.

Answer the following questions:

How do you decide what new work gets done?

What do you do with the backlog?

What system do you use to problem solve?

How many people have to change their roles and responsibilities?

How will you roll out their changes?

> Ideally you want to start with a group of people who are ready and willing to make the changes. This can serve as your pilot group and be champions of the change when you scale the program.

How will you communicate what is happening (not just the progress)?

This is an ongoing process that requires a flexible mindset in order to adapt to the challenges that show up. Stay true to the process of talking through what is showing up rather than insisting you stick to the "original plan."

Job Analysis

One way to establish priorities and clarity around the job is to do a Job Analysis. If you are a leader, you can do this with your team. Be sure to also do this for yourself with your boss.

Everyone has a job description; however, this does not tell you what your boss sees as a priority.

Let your boss know you want to focus on what is most important in your role at this time. In the meeting, have your job description and performance review in front of you; clarity objectives, goals, and priorities as stated. Find out how your performance will be measured and what is significant for your boss—at this specific point in time.

When doing this with your team, explain the values you find important along with the vision you have for your department. Illustrate and share the top skills needed to be successful in your field. This provides an action plan for you and your team to develop professionally.

After this overview of the Job Analysis, get even more basic and differentiate between activities that are important and those that are urgent. Dwight Eisenhower was the first to make this differentiation and is associated with this statement:

"What is important is seldom urgent, and what is urgent is seldom important."

Next, let's define "important" and "urgent" and talk about each quadrant of this matrix to help you understand how to better plan and focus on the activities that will move you toward your goals.

Priority Matrix

This table represents the four categories that fit of all your activities. Where do you spend most of your time?

Important can be defined as an activity that moves you toward your desired outcomes—personally or professionally. The consequences of not following through are not felt immediately and may take time to show up. Ignoring these activities has a major impact, however, and is often the difference between success and failure.

Urgent usually carries with it a need for immediate attention, and it's usually someone else's agenda. The consequences of not following through can be immediate. This is what many people confuse with "important" because of the immediate consequences.

It takes up a lot of resources like time and energy, stealing from the future and draining away creativity.

You can see in the following matrix which activities go with each category. We will talk about each individually. Quadrant two is highlighted and is at the heart of effective leadership. It contains the priorities for your time.

Where do you spend your time?

1 **Important and Urgent** Crisis Deadlines Health issue	**2** **Important, Not Urgent** Relationships Self-care Planning Strategic thinking
3 **Urgent, Not Important** Procrastination Interruptions Stress mode activation Favors	**4** **Not Important, Not Urgent** Some mail Games Social media interaction Advertising

Quadrant 1: Important and Urgent

These activities consist of deadlines, problems, and crises that carry significant impact and demand your immediate attention. This includes situations you could not have foreseen like health issues and certain crises in your industry, along with unplanned activities that "surprise" you. For example, you "knew" about an inspection but missed the deadlines on your calendar because you were too busy putting out fires, and you end up surprised when they show up.

Because this quadrant carries high emotional energy, if you live here most of the time, you lose perspective. This is when you might escape into Quadrant 4—not important and not urgent activities—to slow down your racing thoughts or high emotion.

Leave time in your day to accommodate a crisis.

Quadrant 2: Important. Not urgent.

This is where you want to spend most of your time and prioritize these activities. The more time you spend here, the less time you will spend in Quadrants 1 or 4. With planning, many deadlines and crises can be eliminated. By spending time here, you will eliminate the procrastination that happens with the fight-or-flight reaction and the thinking mode of perpetual crisis.

Schedule in time—every day—to plan, think, and review, *especially* when you feel busy.

Quadrant 3: Urgent. Not Important.

This is where many people spin their wheels. Because of the "urgency," activities can be mistaken for important. Remember what we've said about distraction and the false sense of urgency that is created by lost focus.

This category of activities begs the question, "Can this be delegated or scheduled for a later date?"

These tasks usually come from someone else's agenda and include returning certain phone calls, most emails, text messages, and requests from staff and family members. These activities can be planned for and then will carry the priority based on your daily calendar.

Super Tip

1. Plan for those staff requests to talk about issues.

There are usually one or two individuals who seem to want more of your time. Plan for this and meet regularly with them; learn to set boundaries when they approach you and schedule their requests, so you stay in charge of how you spend your time and energy.

2. Learn to delegate and follow up.

Make it a goal to reduce the time you spend in this quadrant and give this time to Quadrant 2.

Quadrant 4: Not urgent. Not important.

This quadrant is where people go to waste time. It could be because they do not know what is important or because they do not care. This is not the category for unwinding that is Quadrant 2. Mindless activity, goofing off, gossip, searching the Internet, and scrolling through social media under the guise of research not only waste the organization's time but also squander your own career capital because they drain confidence and energy. People are energized when they are productive.

When you schedule in downtime, you will not have to "steal" it and waste more time than is needed to recharge.

Do an audit of your own priorities and how you spend your time. Be truly honest. Learning to make these distinctions and plan your time will dramatically reduce the energy drain you feel from the false state of urgency.

What percentage of time do you spend in each quadrant?

1. Do an inventory of your activities.

2. Then estimate the time you spend in those activities

3. Sort them into the categories on the Priority Matrix.

Important and Urgent % Time spent	**Important, Not Urgent** % Time spent
Urgent, Not Important. % Time spent	**Not Important, Not Urgent** **% Time spent**

Status Quo

The status quo is a problem we all have experienced and accept at some point in time. How is the status quo born? We have been conditioned to think in a certain way and to accept things as being a certain way; this is the nature of families, cultures, and organizations. Most organizations have their sacred cows—the untouchable subjects, protocols, people that continue to operate within the system without any scrutiny.

This conditioning creates the mind's default mode and anything outside of it is resisted. As you build on your ability to think deliberately and strategically, you will go beyond this status quo thinking.

Remember, the stress reaction is a survival instinct designed to keep your attention on a potential threat—real or imagined. This shuts down the ability to consider options. The status quo can be persuasive, as those who want to maintain it, and will offer up justifications to keep everything the same.

Have you ever heard (or said) "If it ain't broke, don't fix it"? Granted, not every problem needs to be fixed. Having a problem-solving system in place will help you deal with problems that show up.

Cultivating a resilient mindset is the antidote to status quo.

Most people fear change because they are not sure how the change will ultimately affect them. Underneath this fear are two questions people have, even if they do not openly ask. Being able to resolve these two issues will go a long way to get beyond resistance. The two questions are:

1. Can I handle it? Do I have the skills needed with this new change?

2. What's in it for me? How will this benefit me?

Talk this through with your team and answer these questions. This is the underlying resistance that stalls progress.

Resilient achievers thrive in a culture of continuous learning and set up a "new normal" that challenges the status quo in search for something better. Here are three questions you can use with yourself, and your team to stimulate fresh thinking:

1. What if we...?

2. What would it take...?

3. How can we...?

Once the questions are asked, take a deep breath, and listen. Do not be afraid of silence. Bring your team into the conversation.

Keep in mind, the status quo mindset exists at all levels in an organization. There are sacred cows that are not talked about. You cannot force anyone to see things differently.

Change their experience and you will change their mind.

Office Politics

Drama is draining. Do you agree?

This is what most people complain about—the "politics" of the workplace: gossip, popularity contests, excessive competition, bullying, and the battle to be heard and understood drain energy faster than anything else. Workdays are longer and harder with this toxic behavior contributing to low productivity and low morale.

The cost of low productivity to the organization is in the billions with staff turnover, error, risk, and poor outcomes. The defensive patterns of drama derail teamwork, collaboration, and destroy productivity.

There are three "drama" conversations that take place. Without self-awareness, this conversation becomes a vicious cycle, and you end up switching roles, going from victim to persecutor. These conversations perpetuate powerlessness and avoid accountability. They are the result of an indirect style of communication in the culture.

These patterns are defense mechanisms that allow each person to keep the status quo alive. Most of the time, these patterns are unconscious; they come from a set of beliefs (with emotional cues) that undermine one's self-confidence and self-image. The way out is through awareness and development of skills in emotional intelligence: assertiveness, emotional expression, impulse control, and resilience.

Let's look at each conversation individually.

"Poor Me"

This conversation comes from a "Victim" persona, feelings of hopelessness and helplessness. The intent of this conversation is to block decisions and interfere with problem solving and progress moving forward.

This conversation needs a "Rescuer" to jump in to save the day in order to keep the cycle going.

Here is an example:

Marta was working late because she took off earlier in the day. Rather than owning this time off, she complained to her co-worker how her boss was so demanding. The new person overheard her and jumped in to "rescue" Marta. She agreed to do the report so Marta could go home early.

Later her co-worked felt manipulated and began blaming Marta for taking advantage of her. While that may be true, this happened because this person felt compelled to rescue someone.

Do you know how to set boundaries or stand up for yourself?

"I Will Save the Day"

The "Rescuer" helps even when they do not want to and ends up feeling resentful. The person feels guilty when they do not help and experiences positive self-worth by helping others. This cycle enables failure rather than accountability. It blocks empowerment and ownership.

Often times the rescuer gets "approval" from people at work because they are picking up the slack. This can set up a major resentment problem when this person wakes up and realizes they have been taking on more responsibility than they should.

"It's Your Fault"

This cycle of destructive communication starts with the blaming, shaming, and criticism from a "Persecutor." Despite the confrontational tone of this conversation, this person is coming from a powerless position, as are the other two.

Think back to Marta and her coworker. The new co-worker reacted to hearing Marta complain and maybe had her own needs to get approval or feel like she belonged and decided to take up Marta's work. This is fine if you are aware of the motivation behind what you are doing.

This type of conversation happens outside of people's awareness is born out of an inability to speak directly about you need and want.

The motivation behind these three roles is to avoid expressing needs and or wishes directly. By relying on these defenses, you focus on protecting your own needs (versus dealing with the needs of the group for the greater good). This can happen when the primitive survival instinct of the fight-or-flight reaction gets triggered; it is easy to lose perspective and react to fears that come up.

As you increase resilience and strengthen emotional intelligence, you avoid these destructive patterns.

Next, take the Drama Quiz.

Drama Self-check

Read through the questions. Answer using a 1 to 10 scale with 10 being "All the time," and 1 being "Rarely." Keep in mind, just about everyone does some of this some of the time.

Your goal is to increase your awareness of your communication style. Be honest in your assessment. It's important to understand your underlying feelings, like powerlessness or anger, that may be the source of this communications style.

1 2 3 4 5 6 7 8 9 10

Rarely   **All the Time**

1. Do you provide unsolicited advice?

2. Do you jump to help even when not asked?

3. Do you compromise to avoid conflict and feel resentful or withdraw from the process?

4. Do you use intimidation to get your way?

5. Are you impatient when things do not go your way?

6. Do you take feedback as a personal attack?

7. Do you feel like you are the only one committed to the project and get frustrated with others?

8. Do you withhold your feelings or opinions because you feel like they won't matter?

Your Score: _____

The higher your score, the greater the chance you are engaging in the drama roles of victim, rescuer, or persecutor. What stood out to you as you went through the questions?

What will you do differently?

Managing Expectations (Setting Boundaries)

To manage expectations means you influence someone's belief about what they expect to happen. At work you have to manage your customers' expectations, employees, and your boss. Unfortunately, it doesn't work that smoothly most of the time. There can be many unknowns when delivering your product or service. You need a strategy to manage expectations.

Expectations are influenced by what you believe, what you have experienced in the past, assumptions, pressures, other people, external messaging, work related goals and priorities. It is up to you to manage expectations, in order to have healthy and fulfilling relationships, success at work, and less stress along the way.

One problem with expectation is *we expect other people* to know what we have going on!

Expectations can create drama and increase the stress reaction, if they are not managed.

Let's start with managing *your* expectations. We have talked about self-awareness; this is a critical element to having success. Here are the steps to manage your expectations:

Step 1: Know what you want. Be honest with yourself.

Whether it is personal or professional, know your desired outcome, make sure it is measurable, so you know when you have achieved it. Be sure to explain it to the other person or group and check to make sure they understand it.

Step 2: Do not make assumptions.

Managing expectations is challenging with people you do not know, and sometimes, even harder with those you know. If you know someone, you assume you know what they want and like. Open your mind, be aware of the potential biases you might have, avoid assumptions.

Step 3: Listen, ask, understand.

Take the time to ask questions, listen, and ask more questions in order to understand what the other person wants. What are their expectations? How soon do they want it and what type of communication do they like and expect around this issue? Do this with people you do not know well and those you do.

Step 4: Be present to what is going on within you, and around you.

Mindfulness helps you avoid emotional hijacking or being caught off guard by emotional reactions, yours or someone else's. It will also help you get in touch with what you really want.

It is natural to have expectations for how things turn out; the challenge comes when you insist other people meet those expectations. Make the time to build trust in the relationship to negotiate these expectations.

Managing Others' Expectations

If you are a business owner, you want to meet and exceed your customer's expectations, to stand out in the marketplace. As an employee you want to manage expectations of your boss, so you do not get overloaded with work, and continue to perform at high standards. As a leader, you need to manage your staff and your customer's expectations. And they will probably be different.

The same is true in personal situations, it is important to manage what other people expect of you, so you can avoid misunderstanding and conflict.

Successful expectation management requires you are consistent in meeting your goals and satisfying those people who are invested in your performance. When your performance becomes dependable, you build trust.

Here are guidelines to help you manage other people's expectations.

1. Communicate. Communicate. Communicate.

Too often plans fail or expectations are not met because there was not enough communication in the planning stage about what is important, when, and how it gets delivered.

Since no two people receive messages in the same way, you want to clarify that what people heard, is what you said, and meant. Avoid confusing and conflicting messages; be direct.

And if you are unsure. Ask. You can always follow up your conversation with, "Did that make sense to you? Let's confirm what is being agreed upon."

2. Anticipate what other people may want.

This is not trying to read their mind. By asking questions, clarifying their answer, you can help the other person identify their needs, and you will be able to anticipate what might work for them. Very often, someone may want something for you but are not clear on the deliverables. Help them figure it out by asking questions.

This is very helpful in work-related situations. Being able to solve your customers (or bosses) problems makes you indispensable.

This is also true for personal situations, ask questions, use examples, clarify, and understand what is expected.

3. Design your feedback loop.

How will you handle communication flow, feedback, boundaries for your workload, uncertainty, mix ups?

Successful interventions are designed within a system that includes the types of interaction, modes of communication needed, and what happens when there are conflicts, or a need for revision.

I use an agile lean framework that will make the process visual. I will incorporate Kanban boards, a variety of meeting and report formulas to discuss progress and gain agreement on the timeline. This can also be applied to personal situations!

When you have a personal situation, it pays to go through this level of planning; it will ultimately save you distress.

Use project planning tools that includes a calendar with timelines, tasks and accountability. This can be communicated with everyone in the preferable format, text, email, or through a virtual connection on a laptop.

By working out a system to deal with the various details of the project, you strengthen the relationship in the process.

Boundaries

Boundaries are easy to spot in the physical world: people put up fences, close the door, pull down the shades, and define their own spaces.

Setting boundaries with people can be a tough lesson, especially if the following questions are running in the background:

> 1. Can I set limits and still be a nice person?

2. What if my limits make it hard on someone else?

3. Is it selfish to set limits?

4. If I am supposed to set limits, why do I feel so guilty?

It is harder to set intangible emotional boundaries. Many of my clients who strive to be a "Servant Leader," find boundaries very difficult to set because of what they think is expected of them under this type of leadership.

Setting boundaries is critical to be effective. Take the quiz below to evaluate your boundary setting.

Boundary Quiz: How Well Do You Set Boundaries?

Rate yourself on the following statements using the "1-to-10" scale, one being never and ten being always.

1. It is hard for me to decide.

2. It is hard to look people in the eye.

3. It is hard to take care of myself.

4. I take care of others and have little left for myself.

5. I am embarrassed and feel different from other people.

6. I do not spend time alone.

7. I cannot keep secrets.

The higher the score, the more difficulty you have in setting boundaries.

Question 1 speaks to the intrusion of other people's beliefs, thoughts, and feelings into their own and the difficulty in knowing what they really prefer.

Question 2 is about feeling bad about who you are, worried others can see right through you. When you have healthy boundaries and feel good about yourself, you can look people in the eye and not worry about getting lost or being seen for who you are. Do you struggle with the Imposter Syndrome?

Questions 3 and 4 are about other people taking up so much space in your own emotional world, there is no room for your own needs. Your sense of accomplishment comes through caretaking others.

Question 5 speaks to the loss of boundaries in defining who you are. When one becomes enmeshed with others, your own uniqueness can feel wrong or bad.

Question 6 speaks to being out of touch with yourself and your inner life. When you are spending your time and energy looking outside of yourself, it is the equivalent of rejecting yourself. When you do finally spend time alone, you may be overwhelmed with critical self-talk and emotions.

Question 7 relates to an all-or-nothing approach to communicating what is going on. You may have had early messaging about holding back and guarding what you feel, so you do not disclose anything. On the other hand, family secrets can become toxic and blurting everything out is your way to balance.

Setting and maintaining boundaries becomes easier as you learn to acknowledge your emotions and listen to their wisdom.

A Toxic Workplace (and Ten Signs of a Healthy One)

Have you ever felt like calling in sick because you did not want to face a coworker who is negative and complains all the time? Maybe you had a boss that micro-manages and it feels humiliating to be told what to do all the time?

Now, think about a time you went to a business setting where you were welcomed, made to feel you mattered and most everyone was kind and greeted you with a smile? This doesn't just happen because of personalities. It is built in to the culture.

This is the difference between a toxic workplace and one that is healthy. Healthy workplaces have greater engagement with almost 90% of the workforce less likely to quit (according to the Corporate Leadership Council, 2004). Great engagement in staff cascades through the organization and produces better outcomes and increased quality.

Not too long ago, my husband had surgery. From the time we went to the surgeon's office to the time of discharge, we were treated like we were the only patient they had that day. There were complications after the operation and not everything went smoothly. What made this a good experience despite the complications was the level of communication and care that everyone exhibited from the physician to the nurses to the aides on night shift. I experienced the kindness of the night shift aide when she brought coffee and blanket. This made a memorable experience.

It was clear that communication was coordinated from the top level of administration down throughout the ranks of the frontline staff. Rounds were held every day; short, stand-up meetings helped the team identify their priorities and identified problems. I saw the executives, managers, physicians, and ancillary staff interacting throughout the day on the unit. The working relationship was obvious; the frontline was very much integrated into the bottom line. The executive level was actively part of patient care as demonstrated by their presence on the unit.

Now let's look at the signs of a toxic workforce and explore what happens in an unhealthy environment.

Seven Signs of a Toxic Workplace

1. Bullying is accepted
2. Unfair workload
3. Gossip predominates
4. Deadlines missed, productivity suffers
5. Use of fear or intimidation to coerce employees
6. Staff or managers covering for each other rather than openly addressing performance issues
7. Status quo mindset

Most people want to do a good job at work. So, what happens?

We have been talking about the elephants in the room; ignoring the daily hassles people experience on the job or the unresolved conflict that wears people down are big fat elephants that destroy a culture.

Frontline staff crave leaders who truly understand and care about them, will mentor them, and will provide professional guidance and the moral strength to make fair and tough decisions. All leaders can exercise a positive influence if they learn to operate from their authentic cores, versus through chronic stress in a fight-or-flight mode.

Toxic environments can seem overwhelming to change and, too often, people go quiet and stay in their own world of responsibility. Everyone contributes to the toxic workplace, including those who ignore it. This is the slippery slope of status quo.

Question: What can you do, daily, to contribute to a healthy workplace?

Let's look at the characteristics of a healthy workplace. Simply:

A healthy workforce produces.

Employee satisfaction is important but that alone does not produce a healthy workplace. The organization is operating to provide a product or service, make a profit (even if it is nonprofit), and demonstrate longevity (outlive their competition). This requires a commitment to performance and relationships.

Below is a list of ten attributes of a healthy workplace. Check off those you agree with and add in those you believe should be on the list.

Ten Signs of a Healthy Workplace

1. Emphasis on positive communication
2. Commitment to excellence, high standards
3. Sense of humor
4. Trust throughout the organization
5. Open communication
6. Respect and civility for each other
7. Collaboration
8. Recognition of well-being's link to performance
9. Balance in work, play, and family
10. Decisive and flexible leadership

Chapter Summary: Why Can't I Get Anything Done at Work?

» Resilient thinking can be developed with awareness and practice.

» These are common stressors at work:

1. *Not enough time*

2. *Too much to do and lack of priorities*

3. *Status quo*

4. *Office politics and drama*

» Use the Priority Matrix and find where you might be leaking time and draining energy.

» Drama can result from a runaway stress reaction. Take the drama quiz.

Study Group Activity

» Consider the following: What do you think it costs your department when staff stop caring about their job/performance? Write it out in your journal and hold a discussion with your group.

» Have your group rank the four challenges for themselves. Discuss this. Challenge each other's "excuses."

» Visualize your workflow.

» Map out your daily activities on the Priority Matrix. Are you spending enough time planning and preventing those "urgent crisis" that derail your best plans?

» Does workflow need to change?

» Use the Keywords, posting one word per week.

Self-awareness is like peripheral vision; you are aware of what is going in you, and how you impact others.

Chapter 6
Emotional Agility

The capacity that got you here, will not get you where you need to go. Resilience and emotional intelligence expand your capacity.

The following are key elements of Ei. These are discussed in this chapter.

1. *Self-Awareness.*
   Do you know your emotions, values, and goals? Do you have an inventory of your strengths and weaknesses and know the impact you have on others?

2. *Focus*
   Did you know your attention is your most

important asset? It is what helps you manage your energy and self-regulate.

3. *Confidence*
How you see yourself is critical to being balanced in your interaction with others.

4. *Optimism.*
This shapes your attitude toward problems and challenges.

Score your emotional awareness on a scale of one to ten?

1   2   3   4   5   6   7   8   9   10

unaware   somewhat aware   very aware

Self-Awareness: The Foundation of Effectiveness

The one key skill that is consistently identified among the most effective leaders is self-awareness. And yet, most leaders do not spend enough time truly analyzing their strengths, areas for improvement, weaknesses, and how they can improve. There is a tendency to overestimate their performance and underestimate the feedback they get from others. In other words, growth stops.

Houston, we have a problem. When you adopt the resilient mindset, you are recognizing that *you* hold the key to work life satisfaction and your success—not your circumstances.

Self-awareness is what allows you to go from good to great.

Resilient thinkers are not distracted by talent or success any more than by failure. The problem with success is that it often stops the process of continued learning and growth. I had a client who continued to brag about her accomplishments despite key missteps that cost her a promotion; she resisted looking closely at where she was now and what she needed to learn to be truly great. She was stuck.

Remember the status quo can kick in at any level. Self-awareness keeps you learning.

Being self-aware is the foundation of emotional intelligence and one of the skills you want to develop. Here is where investing in assessments and coaching will pay dividends that will surpass the small investment.

Super Tip:

Keep a notebook of the feedback you receive. Jot down examples of when you exhibited that behavior. Do this for positive and negative behaviors. Review the positive feedback when you need a boost. Use the negative feedback to schedule in training or coaching to up level those skills.

Awareness keeps you poised to take advantage of opportunities and decreases the chance of overreacting. It will build confidence and set you apart from others.

The Power of Focus

Success is directly related to your ability to focus. Your attention is your most important asset.

In the Age of Distraction, everything is competing for our attention, and the inability to focus has become quite a disadvantage.

Do you know what is most important for you to focus on at work? Do you have priorities for your family? Are you clear on your values? Have you defined your personal goals? Getting clear takes time. I highly recommend you set aside time to think this through. When you are clear about what is important and what you need to focus on, it is easier to say no, and set priorities.

Here are a few strategies to support focus:

1. Evaluate your habits. Do you have habits that are aligned with your goals? Most of your daily behavior is automatic and based on habits. Too often, these habits cost you precious time

and energy. Getting derailed because you stayed up late again and now can't focus on what is in front of you is a habit you can change.

2. Spend time every day unplugged. Interruptions from text, instant messages, and other bells and alarms from the phone make it very difficult to focus.

   Keep an Interruption Log for three days and notice how often you interrupt yourself by checking email or social media. Distraction is a habit. Build your focus muscles.

   Check Appendix for Interruption Log.

3. Use visualization to see yourself achieving your goal. Set up fifteen to thirty minutes at the start of every day to pray, feed your spirit, read inspiration, define your priorities for the day, and visualize your goals.

4. Get the help you need. If you are crunched for time, what can you hire out, so you can focus on your biggest priority? Hire a cleaning service, painter, landscaper, or other services so you can enjoy time with your family. What can you delegate and or train your assistant to do so you can focus on what really matters at work? Way too often, the reason delegation doesn't work is because of poor

communication. When you delegate, be clear and concise when you state your expectations.

5. Avoid the "If Only" trap. Rumination over what might happen will waste your time and drain your energy. It will dampen your desire to find creative solutions. This trap is also rooted in regrets. Work on building good habits, and you will not have to spend time focusing on what "coulda, shoulda, woulda" happened.

Confidence (and What to Do About Confidence Killers)

Confidence can be described as your self-belief, how well you handle setbacks, criticism, and challenge. Do you need validation from others? Do you feel worthwhile?

Confidence is supported by an optimistic attitude, the ability to embrace challenge and your commitment to see a challenge through to the end.

Men and women experience confidence differently. Many women tend to feel a high level of confidence is "presumptuous," whereas men will easily see themselves achieving higher levels of success, despite a lack of ability.

Women run the risk of the "Impostor Syndrome," a form of self-doubt, despite obvious examples of success. Women seem to think they must constantly prove their abilities, a symptom of Impostor Syndrome.

Women are more likely to attribute their success to luck, how they look, or something outside of themselves rather than own their skills and abilities. This difference in self-confidence between men and women is well noted. Women have been shown to hold lower expectations for themselves as compared to men.[11]

Is this why women hesitate to go for the promotion or speak up in meetings? It is not hard to see the impact this has on confidence. This is true for women at all levels of the ladder.

What more might you achieve if you lost your self-doubt?

Confidence develops over time, and it is context specific. You can feel confident professionally but not so much in your personal life. Being distracted will challenge your feelings of confidence.

Being confident and acting confident can also be different. This is what can happen when someone has the ability but lacks belief in themselves; they have a hard time getting others to listen to their ideas. The opposite can happen; someone may lack the ability but hold a very high belief in themselves. This shows up with someone bluffing and charming their way through the activity.

When you have a balanced view of your ability along with self-belief you have what I call, authentic confidence. This includes a sense of humor; you can set boundaries and do not feel like you have to prove something, and you can let others' take the lead if this is best for the desired outcome.

Having confidence does not mean you do not experience fear; it means fear does not stop you from moving forward.

Confidence also lives in your body. How you stand, sit, and hold your head and shoulders will make (or break) your confidence.

Think about a time when you felt confident. How did you experience this in your body? Recreate this experience and practice it. This is especially powerful when you are speaking to a group.

Notice how you feel in your body when you are most confident Write it out in your journal.

Confidence Killers

- Over-preparing
- Self-doubt
- Need to please
- Perfectionism
- Over-belief in luck

- Distraction
- Self-criticism
- Judgment
- Refusing a challenge
- Holding a grudge

Optimism: A Precursor to Resilient Thinking

> ... *the purpose of resilient thinking is to find creative, new ways to provide value. This can't happen if all you see are problems* ...

Optimism is a very important aspect of resilience. Researchers asked Special Forces instructors if their soldiers tended to be more optimistic than pessimistic. The answer was resoundingly, "Optimistic." They noted how contagious an attitude is and said they could not afford risking the entire team's attitude if one of them became negative.[12]

As a leader, do you have a standard for attitudes? What if you required your team to be optimistic to work with you?

While genetics play a role in whether you are naturally optimistic—just like with high blood pressure and diabetes—there are things you can do every day to increase your optimism.[13] Increasing your awareness of your self-talk will help you increase positive thoughts and refute negative ones. Throughout this book are strategies that help you do this.

Become an observer of your conversations. If you feel worried, fearful, or have more doubt, you are focusing on the problem rather than the solution. Resilient leaders acknowledge the problem and spend more time on the solution. This is empowering for you and everyone around you.

Some people define optimism as a *Pollyanna*, "everything is fine" attitude. This definition captures only part of what optimism really is. You need to have a positive outlook to have the motivation to find the solution; however, you also need to have a realistic perspective in order to identify those challenges and be prepared for them.

Optimism enables you to balance the pressure of the challenge with your ability to get through it. An optimistic attitude is easier to have when you are clear and focused and define the problem. These are additional dimensions within emotional intelligence, and they will all contribute to your ability to activate resilience.

In *Leading with Honor*, Lee Ellis talks about the ability to be realistic in his experience as a POW at the "Hanoi Hilton." Those who recognized the serious nature of their capture were able to live through the situation.[14] Those who were continually expecting to be released did not handle the disappointment well and did not survive.

When you are optimistic you can still be realistic about the severity of the challenge ahead of you. Optimism is not an emotion; it is an attitude that can be learned and cultivated.

Optimism requires confidence in oneself to handle the challenges that show up. Confidence increases as you meet those challenges. It is necessary to keep going despite mistakes, failure, and difficulty. A resilient mindset is the direct result of continuing to get back up after every challenge versus playing it safe and staying in your comfort zone.

Quick Steps to Reboot Optimism

1. Observe your self-talk
2. Notice the impact others have on you
3. Be realistic and acknowledge challenges
4. Focus on the solution while having a strategy in place for the problem
5. Remain hopeful

Emotions Are Part of Your Survival Kit

For too many, emotions are the black box in the aircraft. You look at them only when there has been a crash or a tragedy. Emotions are the driving force behind thoughts, beliefs and behavior. It is natural to have a stream of thoughts running in the background of your mind that are triggered by emotions. These generally are ignored.

It is estimated we have between 50,000 and 80,000 thoughts per day, and they include fears, self-doubt, and negative self-talk. To deal with these thoughts, you must be aware they are there, so you can dismiss those that are not aligned with where you want to go. Awareness allows you to shift into a mindset that will take you to your goal.

Because of many of these assumptions (old beliefs), emotions get ignored. Do you subscribe to any of these?

- Emotions should be neither seen nor heard
- It is impossible to manage them, so it is best to ignore them
- Emotions get in the way of strategic decisions
- Emotions are a sign of weakness
- Emotions are not safe

How many times have you said, "I keep my emotions in check!" And how many times do you find yourself overreacting, falling flat in a conversation, or at a loss for empathy?

Damasio, researcher and author on emotions, defines emotions as "complicated collections of . . . responses, . . . [with a] regulatory role to play . . . to assist the organism in maintaining life."[15] He acknowledges that emotion and reason are related; in other words, we all come equipped with a collection of emotions as part of our survival kit.

In other words, emotions are hardwired and necessary for our survival. Darwin found emotions were expressed in a similar way across cultures. Emotions ensure survival. The message that "one can separate one's emotions and still function well" is a myth. We are biologically hardwired to use emotional cues to make decisions and get through our day. Survival depends on the recognition of emotional cues.

Physically, the limbic system is where emotions live in the brain. About the size of a walnut, the limbic system is made up of parts of the brain involved in emotional memory and motivation. Structures such as the amygdala, olfactory bulb, and hippocampus (to name a few) play an important role in the expression of emotions. This region of the brain, sometimes called the "feeling" brain, sits underneath the cortex, or the "thinking brain."

The size of the cortex might imply power over the smaller structures of the brain; however, as we mentioned before, the survival instinct of the primitive brain triggers an emotional hijacking, and the cortex cannot stop it.

The fact is, we are hardwired to feel first, and then think.

Emotional Hijacking (The Runaway Stress Reaction)

If your nervous system was an operating system, there has not been an upgrade in 100,000 years. When stress is chronic and the ability to withstand stress (resilience) is underdeveloped, there are several consequences, such as the loss of emotional control, slower information processing, and a decrease in working memory, impacting long-range planning and creativity.

Under stress, the amygdala—the part of the brain that monitors the environment for fear-inducing stimuli—is triggered, swamping more rational thought processes. This is the fast track of the stressed response.

Stress tolerance means you operate more from your higher function of your brain (cortex) and avoid triggering the primitive survival instinct of the amygdala.

This is focus. This allows for systematic, methodical processing, critical thinking, and an evaluation process, making decisions better through-out.

Stress tolerance *does not* mean you take whatever comes at you without flinching!

Chronic, unmanaged stress interrupts the ability to think clearly, remember, and retrieve important data. This is hard-wired physiology, and the impact of too much cortisol circulating through your body. Many, in hindsight, recognize that stress contributed to decisions that were not well thought-out or to emotional reactions uncharacteristic of their usual behavior. They are left with the challenge of damage control because of their reactions and poor decisions.

How much time is wasted on repairing the fallout from hijacked reactions? Have you lost relationships because of being hijacked?

When you cannot think straight under pressure you will undermine teamwork, morale, and successful outcomes, adding to the pressure. This problem can be prevented by learning to identify your emotions.

Emotional Awareness (Name It and Tame It)

Most people go through their day locked into a habitual pattern of reacting. It is only when you begin to question your reactions and emotions that you begin to understand what you are feeling and why. Research shows that when you can identify your emotion, give it a name, you are able to slow your reaction.

Naming your emotion allows you to tame it.

Take a moment and reflect on the history of your emotional patterns. In reflecting you can breakthrough any patterns that no longer work for you.

This exercise is a great introduction to your emotions. These exercises build self-awareness.

To help you tune in and become more aware of your emotional experiences, evaluate the following questions:

Anger · Happiness · Anxiety · Fear · Sadness

1. Look at the 5 feelings above. What feeling is usually most intense for you using a 1-10 scale?

   0 _____ 10

Feeling: _____

2. What feeling is most frequent on a 1-10 scale?

   0 _____ 10

Feeling: _____

3. What is the typical outcome as a result of this feeling? Does it impact your relationships, job, energy levels, or motivation? Write this out in your journal.

Anger

Anger is an important emotion. I want you to get to know your anger. When ignored, anger turns to rage, resentment, heart disease, and worse, it shuts down your ability to be happy and enjoy your life.

Remember, emotions are neither good nor bad. They are designed to inform you.

What Anger Is Telling You

Remembering that all emotions are designed to flow and inform, know that anger alerts you to set boundaries and facilitate change. That could be simply putting your hand up and saying, "Stop," when someone is attempting to force you to do something you do not want to do or talking at you and disrespecting your space.

Anger is a universal emotion that has cultural and gender differences. Women are more than likely taught to hold it in, while men are taught to express it. Some people see anger as a masculine emotion.

Most people deny their anger for a variety of reasons. When this happens, you can count on it showing up at the worst possible time. Like all emotions, anger is an internal signal to take some sort of action.

Denying your anger can increase the use of sarcasm, passive-aggressive behaviors, and other mixed signals, decreasing your ability to communicate clearly. The reflection exercise on the previous page will help you be aware of when anger shows up and its impact on you and the people around you.

Techniques introduced chapter eight, when practiced regularly, will help you transform your anger.

Use your journal and write out the answers to these questions about anger:

How do you know you are angry? What do you feel in your body?

What happens as a result of experiencing anger?

How does it affect other people?

How does it interfere with your goals?

How would you prefer to experience anger?

Who or what flips your anger switch on?

Happiness

Happiness is an individual experience. Thousands of years ago, Aristotle recognized that more than anything, people sought happiness. People seek happiness for its own sake. It can be an experience that defies words.

Defining happiness is difficult, and people often start out by saying what happiness is not. It is not having all the money or time in the world. It is doing something meaningful. It is not feeling good all the time nor is it a destination. It is fleeting, elusive, and takes time. Trying too hard gets in the way of happiness.

Happiness is on a continuum and includes feeling cheerful, satisfied, content, as well as optimistic. It is personal.

Boredom is a barrier to happiness. And boredom is telling you to stretch yourself, grow, and learn something new. Happiness is best achieved in the act of reaching for a goal and doing something you did not think you could do.

Be sure to reflect on the questions and journal your answers. The more you cultivate happiness, the less likely you will get stuck in an emotional storm.

Use your journal and write out the answers to these questions about happiness:

How do you know you are happy? What do you feel in your body?

What happens as a result of experiencing happiness?

How does it enhance your goal?

What would it take to experience more happiness?

What experiences flip your happiness switch on?

Anxiety

Fear, when chronic and generalized, becomes anxiety. Anxiety arises from thoughts. It can catch you in an endless thought loop. Did I sign off on that contract? Did I forget something? What if *xyz* happens—what then? And on and on and on. Many people I talk to experience this type of endless questioning at the end of the day.

What Anxiety Is Telling You

Anxiety, when not chronic, can serve as a messenger to help you clarify a situation, so you can take action.

When anxiety becomes chronic, it can be the body's way of avoiding something. Chronic anxiety shrinks your world in the effort to avoid feeling the anxiety. Phobias become a way of coping with the anxiety.

Anxiety, as part of the fear emotion, wants you to take some sort of action. Much of the anxiety people experience results from constant distractions and not being able to remember what they've done. Use your phone to create lists or download one of the many apps that will help you stay organized and focused.

Be sure to reflect on the questions and journal your answers.

Use your journal and write out the answers to these questions about anxiety:

How do you know you are anxious? What do you feel in your body?

What happens as a result of experiencing anxiety?

How does it interfere with your goal?

What would you like to experience instead?

Who or what flips your anxiety switch on?

Fear

Fear is triggered by your primitive part of the brain, the amygdala, the alarm system in your nervous system hardwired to protect us from danger. It is instinctive, and the reaction happens instantaneously. The amygdala sends the trigger to the hypothalamus, which then creates the physiological patterns for that fear. Your heartrate can go up, and you might feel a lump in your throat, tension in your neck, numbness in your hands, and any number of other physical reactions. This reaction is stored to be used over and over when something close to this experience happens.

Fear triggers the fight-or-flight response in the stress reaction. Your amygdala is the storehouse of all your fear experiences (even those you forget) and responds immediately when it senses an experience like what has been stored. Most of the time, people are not aware of the origin of their fear and may not be consciously aware of their reaction.

Using these stress strategies presented in this program will help you overcome the instinctive pull of this primitive reaction. Fears are usually specific to a person, place, or situation and arise from feelings.

Use your journal and write out the answers to these questions about fear.

How do you know you are fearful? What do you feel in your body?

What happens as a result of experiencing fear?

How does it interfere with your goal?

What would you like to experience instead?

Who or what flips your fear switch on?

Sadness

Sadness is not the same as depression, although it is frequently associated with it. Depression is a more complex experience. There are the clinical definitions of depression—bipolar disorder, postpartum depression, dysthymia, mild depression, atypical depression, and major depression.

Sadness is not the same as grief. Grief shows up in response to losses that are irretrievable. Grief can happen as a result of a physical death or the death of a dream, an opportunity, a period in your life, part of your body—any loss that is gone forever. There are stages of grief, and—as with all emotions—it is best to move through grief, present and mindful to what you are experiencing. Too many people medicate their grief.

I highly recommend having help in moving through grief because one loss will trigger other losses you have experienced, and it quickly can feel overwhelming.

What Sadness Is Telling You

Sadness, with its heaviness, the desire to withdraw, and the need to cry, is a cue you need time to reflect, review your life, and let go of things that are not working. Sadness gives you a window into what you value. This helps you understand yourself better. When you can acknowledge your own sadness, you increase the ability to demonstrate empathy. By acknowledging sadness and moving through it, you develop courage and the ability to do other difficult things. Sadness is like other emotions and is designed to flow. Acknowledge it, and remind yourself, "This too shall pass."

When sadness is not acknowledged and is ignored, you can move into despair, which is a mood and lacks the natural flow built into sadness. Crying can often provide the relief needed to let go, and, with the release of tension, you can relax and begin to restore yourself. You have heard the sayings, "I just need a good cry," or, "Have a good cry, and you will feel better." This wisdom speaks to the cleansing and refreshing nature of moving through sadness.

Get to know how sadness shows up for you; reflect on the questions and journal your answers.

Use your journal and write out the answers to these questions about sadness.

How do you know you are sad? What do you feel in your body?

What happens as a result of experiencing sadness?

How does it interfere with your goal?

What would you like to experience instead?

Who or what flips your sadness switch on?

Fatal Emotions

We have all received some type of disappointing news. Your promotion did not come through, the raise wasn't what you expected, you lost the bid for the job, you did not get accepted into your program—the list can go on.

Disappointment is part of living life. When you do not manage those disappointments and you become discouraged, that can be fatal. Discouragement that goes unchecked destroys self-image, confidence, and expectations for the future.

Discouragement

The dictionary definition of discouragement is "the act of making something less likely to happen." When discouragement is left unchecked, it can grow into a mood, eroding motivation and momentum.

The erosion can be subtle. The discouragement shifts to a feeling that "things will never work out." You may try harder only to experience more disappointment, or you may give up altogether. Either way, discouragement kills drive.

When you can identify your feelings, you will be able to take the right action to shift them.

Go from Discouraged to Determined

1. **Name it:** Whenever you feel disappointment, identify it and act.

2. **Reframe it**: Identify three things that are going well for you.

3. **Claim it**: Engage the optimist in you and recognize that it is not permanent, and things will change. Denial is what makes this emotion fatal, capable of destroying your mojo.

4. **Talk about it:** (Or, write in your journal.) Find a safe person who will simply listen. At this point, talking it out helps release the heavy emotion. You can find solutions later.

5. **Help someone else**: The tendency with discouragement is to narrow your focus and think only of your problems. Get out of yourself and reach out to someone in need.

6. **Move on**: Let it go and focus on your big vision.

In addition to these steps, do something every day to manage the stressful feelings that come up. You will learn proven strategies to activate your resilience, the more you practice these, the stronger your resilience.

Let's talk about the *most* fatal emotion, one that only happens to everyone else denial.

Denial

It is a defense mechanism we *all* use to protect ourselves from some perceived threat. Maybe there was bad news, and you instinctively minimize it to get through the emergency. This temporary use of denial is helpful.

Denial becomes fatal when you use it to avoid dealing with situations that require action. Drinking too much, avoiding dealing with financial strain, avoiding your bullying coworker, or signs your teenager is using drugs, ignoring the fact you are using food to compensate for your disappointments—these are all examples of denial that is fatal.

You can deny your own behavior or that of others. Denying your own behavior shows up in chronic blaming. If you persistently accuse others of doing something wrong, chances are the problem lies with you.

Here is an example. A client came to me distressed and ready to quit her job because her boss was blaming her for misplacing reports in the office. He was disorganized and never put anything away, so piles would grow on his desk. He would call her and accuse her of taking the document and not returning it. She did not want to talk to him about it and decided to avoid any conflict.

It is helpful to realize that in any interaction, both people are responsible for the outcome. Are you contributing to a situation by trying to avoid it?

When you avoid taking any action, you are denying your responsibility in the situation. If you feel like a victim and complain, "Things always happen to me," chances are you are using denial to avoid acting.

Denial allows problematic situations and health risks to continue, ultimately creating more serious issues. If you have been exposed to traumatic events or are reaching exhaustion and you continue to push yourself, the body's ability to adapt reaches its limit and you can hit the wall. It is important to address the signs of burnout long before you crash.

It is important to address issues with your staff and followers before they become a much bigger issue. When denial can operate within a culture, you turn off creativity and initiative. In a culture steeped in denial, people essentially go to sleep.

What beliefs keep you from seeing problems as they show up?

Being realistic and facing the challenge is a characteristic of a high Ei leader.

The value of denial is as a short-term defense mechanism.

Suggestions to Go Beyond Denial

1. Be open to feedback. Before you shut out what someone tells you, consider this: is there any truth to what they are saying?

2. Get in touch with your fears. Does change threaten you? Afraid to succeed? What are your fears?

3. Talk to someone—counselor or coach. Your friends or family are not going to move you ahead. Talk with a professional.

4. Evaluate your life to date. Is it working out the way you expected, or has it fallen short? If so, in what way? Be objective. Have your beliefs held you back? What are they?

5. Journal every day. Use the Daily Review to reflect on what is working and what isn't. Keep this for a year, and you will have a timeline review you can use to evaluate patterns of success, avoidance, progress, or resistance.

Chapter Summary: Emotional Intelligence

» Emotional intelligence is the factor that differentiates great leaders from good ones.

» Self-awareness, focus, optimism, and confidence are key elements in emotion intelligence.

» In the Age of Distraction, everything is competing for our attention, and the inability to focus has become quite a disadvantage.

» Optimism requires confidence in oneself to handle the challenges that show up.

» When you can name you emotions you have more control over them.

» Discouragement and denial are fatal emotions and need to be managed.

Study Group Activity

» Are there certain emotions, group members have more difficulty managing?

» How can the group help members when they become discouraged?

» How should the group deal with a member who is in denial related to work issues?

Be deliberate in thought, word and action.

Chapter 7
Resilient Thinking

The ultimate value of resilient thinking is being able to accomplish your goals and move forward in your career and life. There is so much competing for your attention today, and the constant pull of these urgent distractions makes it so important to have clearly defined goals.

The following characteristics are consistent with resilient thinking:

1. You anticipate change. Are you thinking about the future or waiting to be told the next move?

2. You use both your right and left brain. You use both analytic, logical reasoning and creative processing, like your intuition.

3. You are decisive. You can make decisions rather than getting trapped in analysis paralysis.

4. You are open-minded. You do not judge your own suggestions or the suggestions of or others; you keep your options open. There is a degree of patience as you consider many options instead of rushing to a decision.

5. You learn from mistakes. You review and revise as you go through your day and learn from the things that do not go so well.

6. You recognize you may have bias and listen to others for a different perspective.

High-performance leadership is a decision you make to keep growing. When you choose to embrace your potential, you will empower others to do the same.

Boost Your Resilient Thinking

Ask these questions every week. Keep a journal—online or in a notebook—and write out the answers. Periodically, look back and evaluate yourself. Are you learning and growing?

1. What went right?

2. What went wrong?

3. What did I learn from #1 and #2?

4. What is my top priority for next week?

5. What did I waste time on last week?

6. Am I getting in my own way (self-sabotage)?

7. Why am I doing this?

Keep in mind that high performance and work-life satisfaction is not a destination. It is an ongoing process where you integrate new habits and slowly eliminate habits that don't advance your goals.

Balance may not seem possible at first, so focus on integrating ways you can renew your energy throughout the day. Tune in to your ability to focus and finish, your level of joy and satisfaction, and foundational habits like sleep and hydration. Then, adjust and adapt your routines and your mindset so you can achieve your goals. Support, coaching, and training can make a big difference.

Check out the Resilient Leader program for support in this process. This coaching program offers 1:1 and group support to build skills in emotional intelligence and resilience that will increase confidence and keep you operating from your strengths.

Now that you understand how to activate resilience and strengthen your resilient thinking, what do you want these skills to do for you? Take the time to identify your professional and personal goals.

You Are the Message

Roxanne seemed a natural fit for the leadership role in her professional association. She'd held many positions in leadership, including manager, educator, and director. She knew that running for President of her professional association would take her outside of her comfort zone. She was very used to being out in front of her followers' leading meetings and interacting but stepping out in front of her peers felt different to her.

She sought out coaching to develop an authentic leadership brand because she wanted to run for President of this association and take on new leadership roles.

When she talked about her "style" of leadership, what came through was her need to be liked by her team. She talked about situations where she overaccommodated and had trouble setting boundaries. She thought being "nice" was expressing emotional intelligence.

As Roxanne tried harder to be liked, she was not perceived as confident. A very interesting study found when tone and facial expression do not match the words, tone and facial expression will win out over content.[16] In other words, it is not what you say but how you say it that ends up being communicated.

It was helpful for Roxanne to focus on her strengths and recognize she had the attributes and skills needed to fulfill that role. By focusing on being liked, she sold herself short and frequently felt insecure.

When she shifted her desire to be liked to an attitude of providing value, the transformation was amazing.

Her need "to be liked" shifted to "how can I help my team succeed?" By leveraging this strength, she used her innate instinct to coach. She found the relationships with her team very satisfying. Her need to be liked had been transformed to providing value; she knew was making a difference.

Roxanne developed her capacity for resilient thinking by increasing her awareness of her goals, desires, and natural instincts. As she learned more about herself through coaching, assessments, and reflection, her authentic confidence came through. She was able to shift from being accommodating to helping others improve their skills.

Roxanne learned to embrace her strengths and to deliberately lead through them. I took her through a branding process to own her brand. And when she approached the role of President for her association, she felt more confident and congruent than ever before.

Reflection

Grab your journal and write out your answers to the following:

What (and who) motivates you? What have you learned from them?

What are the values and experiences that contribute to your success?

How can you share more of your inspiration with others?

Resilient Mindset: Check Yourself

Rate yourself on each dimension. Give yourself a 5 if you consistently demonstrate that aspect. Total each column.

RESILIENT THINKING		EVERYDAY THINKING	
Do what's needed.	5 4 3 2 1	Do what's required.	5 4 3 2 1
Focused on solutions.	5 4 3 2 1	Focused on problems.	5 4 3 2 1
Embrace uncertainty.	5 4 3 2 1	Resist change.	5 4 3 2 1
Challenge status quo.	5 4 3 2 1	Challenge the change.	5 4 3 2 1
Lead yourself first.	5 4 3 2 1	Require others to change.	5 4 3 2 1
Give the benefit of the doubt.	5 4 3 2 1	Doubt the good.	5 4 3 2 1
Embrace personal growth.	5 4 3 2 1	See no reason to change.	5 4 3 2 1
Score		**Score**	

Effective leadership begins first with a way of thinking that translates into a way of doing, ultimately leading to a way of being.

What do you need to do every day to stimulate your thinking?

Suggestion:

1. Daily Review

2. Engage mindful attention

What will you commit to?

When you are going through hell, keep going.

—WINSTON CHURCHILL

Chapter 8
Strategies to Activate Resilience

To shift your mindset, you must practice strategies that will unhook you from the reactive nature of the stress reaction. In this section, I outline several strategies that are proven to work within minutes. With regular use, you can build your stress tolerance and resilience "muscle;" this is your ability to maintain peak performance even during stressful situations.

Here are three steps to success:

1. Familiarize yourself with all these strategies. Use them all at least twice.

2. Start using them when you are relaxed and rested.

3. Do something every day, even when you do not feel you need it.

It is important to remember that stress is the new normal and, to become resilient, you will have to practice at least one of these methods on a regular basis. You cannot think your way out of a stress reaction, and when you ignore what can happen, you leave yourself vulnerable to a hijacking.

Let's start with the most basic intervention you can use to change your reaction to stress.

Breathing Techniques

On a Count of Four, Breathe!

This is a very simple practice that will yield powerful results. You are breathing anyway; this is just breathing with intention, and the goal is to shift the stress effect.

Breathing is your first line of defense against the distraction of the stress reaction and overwhelm.

Most people today are in moderate to severe stress, multitasking, or in the throes of strong emotions.

Breathing gets shallow and less effective in blowing off the buildup of CO_2, leaving you more acidic—the opposite of what the body needs to stay energized. This shallow way of breathing becomes a habit.

Start by taking four deep breaths: in on the count of four, hold on a count of four, and exhale on the count of four. Wait four seconds before your next breath. Breathe in through your nose and out your mouth.

Repeat four times.

Deliberate Breathing

Now, breathing normally, think about something for which you are grateful, like the short line at the gas pump, your recent promotion, your health, your grandchildren, your pet, your job—anything that helps you experience the feeling of gratitude, appreciation, or love. You are now speaking the language of the heart, which can bring your nervous system into balance.

Continue this for twenty seconds, longer if possible. Just bring yourself back to the feelings of gratitude and release any thoughts that may try to disrupt your ability to stay in the moment. Work up to three minutes at a time and do these five times a day. This will have cumulative results, building your resilience, increasing your capacity for stress, and improving your focus.

Use a timer so you keep track of time.

Manage Your Energy. Increase Your Time.

We tend to expend more energy than we renew.

Most people go through the day with constant interruptions, irritations, and other emotional triggers, all draining energy. Renewing energy is put off "until" a certain point, which usually doesn't come.

When energy is continually depleted, resilience—or capacity—is also depleted. Science now shows that our body continues to respond to a stressful event hours after the event is over, until you engage an intervention that is specifically geared towards balancing your nervous system.

Think of resilience as your capacity, much like the battery in your cell phone. When you do not recharge it, you cannot use it. Your inner battery requires certain conditions; we are all unique in this way.

Therefore, it pays to be aware of what is happening internally.

Write out the answers to these questions in your journal.

What do you notice when your inner battery is drained?

Are you more irritable?   Yes ☐   No ☐   Maybe ☐

What is your response to physical and mental fatigue?

Low energy leads to mistakes on the job, relationship issues, overeating, burnout, and overall diminished health. When this becomes chronic, it affects sleep—and sleep is a primary way to rejuvenate. This sets up a vicious cycle.

Take a Moment (3-Second Transition)

The present moment is about three seconds. Practice "being in the moment," and breathe intentionally. For example, when you start your day, rather than going through the motions of opening your laptop, turning on the computer, and sipping your coffee, be deliberate instead. Pause, breathe, and think about what you are going to do. Appreciate it, focus on it—for three seconds.

This slows down your mind and opens your awareness. With practice, it will also expand your situational awareness and lead to more enjoyment in your day, sense of satisfaction, improved wellbeing, and appreciation for others.

It starts by taking a moment and being deliberate with three seconds.

When to Use the 3-Second Transition:

1. When getting out of bed. Before you do—breathe, acknowledge your day, and then get up.
2. Before and after any meeting, professional or personal. Open and close the meeting, in your mind, by using three seconds to: (1) acknowledge what is happening, (2) bring your full attention to the meeting, and (3) bring your full attention back to yourself at the close of the meeting.
3. Before and after every meal. Practicing mindfulness while eating is a great way to eat less and enjoy your food more.
4. Before you walk in your front door at home. Clear your mind and refresh your attention.

5. Walking into your office. Breathe deliberately and clear your mind, saying to yourself, "I am ready to focus."
6. Before and after difficult conversations. Keep your attention on what you need to learn about this person or to understand the situation. After the conversation, tune in to your emotions and what you need to do to process any raw emotions.

Homework

Practice Attention Reboot:

You can use a timer initially. Set it for 20 seconds.

> Start by breathing more slowly and deeply than normal and refreshing your mind. Let your thoughts drift. You will be getting back to them shortly.
>
> Continue to breathe and simply notice, without judgement, what is happening in and around you. Now, experience where you are as if it were the very first time you were there.
>
> What was that like?

Researchers have found that people who have learned to savor the moment experience more positive experiences in the course of the day. They found people reported feeling "happier" when they were able to control the wandering of their minds.

Continue to practice being in the moment; notice how your attitude changes, as well as your interactions with other people.

Neuroscience tells us we can learn quickly; our brain rewires itself according to our experience. Mindfulness enhances this plasticity, increasing the ability to balance and buffer stressful experiences.

As an executive, mindfulness becomes one of your main tools to engage your personal change. Mindfulness will increase your awareness, help you stay present, and buffer the stress reaction that comes with increased pressure. Not a bad return on a minutes-a-day practice!

Mindful Attention

Learning to stay in the present is the practice of mindfulness. When you think about the future or worry about the past, you have squandered this precious time.

What can happen in 3 seconds? Think back to conversations that went askew because you missed cues or did not understand what was being communicated. Did you pick up the tone, facial expression, or gestures? Did you overreact to them?

What about the hurtful expression you missed that created misunderstanding? Three seconds is just the amount of time you need to slow down your overreaction and avoid a dramatic situation.

Turn on the cooking shows and look what these amazing chefs do in 3 seconds to meet their challenge!

Distraction Is the New Normal

Do you keep your phone next to you and constantly check for texts, emails, Facebook posts, Twitter, Instagram, and more?

Do you start reading and then realize by the end of the page you do not remember a single word?

Are you listening when someone is talking or thinking of something else and catching only every other word?

Is it hard to focus and finish?

Let's look at a common example of distraction. If you are hungry, most people are going to go search for something to eat. When many people feel anxious, tired, angry, or hurt, they also go in search for something to eat. Before long, just about any feeling can be associated with hunger, and food becomes the universal solution. Eating becomes the antidote for any type of emotional distraction.

So, how do you know if you are hungry or feeling an emotion?

Tuning into what you are feeling requires you first quiet your mind and break free of the distractions. Learning to redirect your attention relaxes your mind and body and ultimately increases your effectiveness. At the end of this section is a meditation to increase your awareness.

Research into the power of the brain now demonstrates, the brain can change in response to what we think, feel, and do. The brain function and structure can change with a regular practice of mindfulness. Research has shown changes in concentration, overall well-being, memory, anxiety, sleep, and self-esteem to name a few of the many benefits of a mindfulness practice.

This neuroplasticity is good and bad. If you keep reacting and doing what you have always done, it is easier to keep doing this. This is how habits are quickly formed when distracted and you continue to operate based on a knee-jerk decision. Mindfulness increases your awareness and will slow down your reactive decisions.

As you go through your busy day wrapped up in thoughts and feelings without a break, you may find it useful to check in. Stop and ask yourself, "What is happening right now, in this moment?"

Engaging in a regular practice of mindfulness will help you develop focus and awareness while enhancing your resilience. You can do this with a few simple shifts in your attention. Keep reading; at the end of this section, I offer up suggestions to incorporate mindfulness during your day.

Mindful Attention Is Deliberately Directing Your Attention

Mindfulness means directing your attention to what is happening in the moment *without judging* what is happening. The practice of mindfulness improves the quality of your attention.

It is called a "practice" because the mind has a steady stream of thoughts, feelings, and questions and quickly goes off track. You have to continually practice developing your attention. Mindfulness is the practice of bringing your focus into the moment while tuning out the competing thoughts and feelings.

This practice increases your ability to focus and decreases your reactivity to stress. As you tune in, you are observing your experience rather than reacting to it. This means you simply notice what you are experiencing without trying to change what you are experiencing.

Start by Setting Your Intention

Intention is where you direct your attention. This is the first step in a mindfulness practice. You must first set a goal that you will be present. Your intention references where you will be directing your attention.

When you are mindful, you are bringing your attention back to your goal, over and over.

1. Set your intention
2. Stay aware of this intention
3. As you notice thoughts, feelings, and other distractions, remind yourself of your intention and redirect your attention.

These three steps are the foundation of your mindfulness practice. Use these to increase your ability to be present and focused during everyday activities.

Keep a journal about your mindfulness practice. Here are a few questions to reflect on:

1. What was the process like to set an intention?
2. What thoughts were the most distracting?
3. When is it easier to be more mindful?

Let's say it is your intention (goal) to be present while you eat. With lives on the go, fast food has become the norm. Over 75% of food that is eaten is processed and already prepared. This is only part of the problem;

this food is eaten in a car, in front of the TV or computer, or while reading. You can double your caloric intake when you eat this way, overeating, as your body does not feel full in time to register what you have eaten.

Next time you eat (and it doesn't matter what you eat), start by taking a few deep breaths: in on a count of four, hold on a count of four, and then out on a count of four. Then, continue to breathe for about ten seconds. This should quiet your mind and help you focus on your food.

As you eat, notice the weight of the food on the fork, or the color, aroma, and textures of the food as you look at it on your plate. Chew each bite and notice what is happening in your mouth as you chew. Just focus on your experience as you eat. It is normal for your mind to wander as you start this practice; simply notice and remind yourself of your intention to be present while you eat, then bring it back to your food.

Eating slower and tuned in to yourself, you will recognize more quickly when you feel satisfied. Stop eating before you feel full. Your stomach digests best when it is two-thirds full. Wrap up the rest of your food and push away from the table. Take a few sips of water to refresh your palette and breathe deeply for ten seconds.

Mindfulness is an exercise you can practice at any time. Use your breath to bring you back to a quiet place so you can keep your attention on what is going on in the moment. Keep your journal handy as you may find yourself gaining insights into your choices and behavior.

Reduce Emotional Hijacking and Runaway Stress Reactions

Today, stress reactions are frequently running in the background because of so many distractions. Distractions increase the sense of urgency and block your ability to focus on what is most important. (Remember the section on the Priority Matrix?)

Think of the brain like a high-performance car; to keep it performing at peak levels, it needs more maintenance than the everyday commuter car that you drive until it dies. This maintenance includes strategies of mindfulness, and journaling. Let me briefly introduce parts of your internal computer (brain) to help you understand why these strategies work.

Let's start with the part of your brain that frequently goes off-line when in a stress mode, the pre-frontal cortex (PFC). It is like a CEO, handling complex functions and insuring you achieve the results you want. Here are the main functions:

- regulating impulses
- emotional reaction
- problem solving
- directing attention
- planning
- dealing with competing distractions
- impacts mood
- motivation
- decision making

The pre-frontal cortex (PFC) links other parts of the brain, the limbic system (emotional center), cortex (thinking center), and brain stem, carrying out complicated functions based on your body's internal direction. A regular practice of mindfulness has been shown to increase activity of the PFC enabling greater ability to tune out distractions and focus on what is most important.

Journal on the following:

1. What happens when your PFC goes off-line?
2. Of the functions listed above, which get derailed most often?
3. What are the triggers?

The other part of the brain that plays a key role in emotional hijacks is the amygdala. This part of the brain plays a key role in processing emotions and controls how we react to certain triggers, especially something that is threatening. The brain does not know the difference between what is real or imagined. Acting like a panic button, the amygdala sounds the alarm and sets the nervous system into motion with perceived threat. This flight or fight reaction is how many people go through their day.

This little almond-shaped structure in the brain holds the memories of all our experiences and reacts when those memories are triggered. Because of how memories are stored, emotional memories are usually stored outside of conscious awareness. These are the memories that can get tripped and create an emotional hijacking.

Regular mindfulness practice will increase clarity and feelings of calm, decreasing the reactivity of your amygdala.

Journal on the following:

1. What triggers cause an emotional hijacking?
2. How do these experiences relate to past experiences?

Suggestions to Apply Mindful Attention

You can incorporate mindfulness into your day through the methods listed below. Choose one to use for a few days then add in others as this practice becomes easier. Consistency with this practice will yield tremendous benefit (versus longer periods of practice done infrequently).

1. Before you get out of bed, take a deep breath. Breathe in gratitude and breathe out frustration. (10 seconds)

2. Drink 6 ounces of water. Notice how you feel after drinking the water. Refreshed?

3. When brushing your teeth, notice the weight of the toothpaste. Any color or smell? What is the temperature of the paste as you brush your teeth? Keep your thoughts on the activity of brushing your teeth. Notice the temperature of the water. How does your mouth feel after brushing? When finished, look at yourself in the mirror and smile!

4. Driving to work. Start with noticing the car: its color, lines; is it dirty or clean? Do you open with a key bob, what is that sound like? Do you press it once or twice? As you slide into the seat, what does the texture feel like?

When you start the engine, how does it sound—running smoothly, any chugging sounds? As you drive to work, keep your thoughts on the driving experience. Notice the cars as they come up on you. Use your mirrors and be fully present to driving. As your mind wanders onto thoughts about what you must do at work, bring your attention back to driving.

Use the word, driving, to keep your attention on this experience.

When you pull into work and park, before you turn off the engine, notice how you feel. Take a deep breath. Are you more relaxed?

5. Meetings. Before you go into the meeting, set an intention to be fully present. As you walk down the hall to the meeting, what do you notice? How are you feeling? Who do you see? What is on the walls, on the floor? What noises or smells are there?

When you get into the meeting, keep your mind on what is happening in the meeting. When your mind wanders to lunch or your vacation or any other subject, bring yourself back to the meeting.

How do you feel when the meeting ends and what did you notice that is new?

6. Eating. Use the mindfulness exercise presented earlier during your meals.

The Body Scan: Quick Check-In

This is useful to check in with your physical body and notice what is going on. This will make you aware of the impact of people, situations, and even food. When are you energized? Tense? Does your energy drag after certain meetings? Tension in your neck, back?

Instructions

Start with the count of 4 breathing: breathe in on a count of 4, hold your breath for 4, and then exhale on 4. Then, breathing slower and deeper than usual, start at the top of your head, and scan all the way down your body to your toes. Notice if there is any tightness, tension, body aches. For now, simply observe what you are feeling. Ask:

- Are there any emotions trying to come through the tension?
- Are you thirsty, hungry, tired, cranky?

If distracting thoughts show up, go back to the scan and just observe what you are experiencing. During the scan, 15 seconds, you are simply observing. Being able to maintain this discipline of mindfulness will slow down your reactions and increase your awareness.

Now that you have noticed something, go back to that spot and keeping your thoughts neutral, breathe more slowly and deeply than usual into that spot, and repeat, "I release and let go."

Do this several times during the day. You will do this automatically after a few weeks of practicing this technique.

You can journal your experience and the thoughts that came up.

Journaling

Taking ten minutes at the start of your day can be special time you spend with yourself. This practice will open you up to parts of yourself that you otherwise would not have the chance to explore. The relief of tension happens quickly as you write out what you have been holding onto inside. This practice will increase self-awareness and build your ability to stay in the moment.

Journaling is one of the most powerful methods to grow personally and professionally. Writing out your thoughts gives you a visual map and helps you stay the course or make needed changes. Learning is quicker with reflection, which engages all your senses and more of your brain. Journaling slows your thoughts and helps you with perspective.

You will know yourself at a deeper level and get to the real motives that drive your choices and behavior.

Types of Journals

1. *Idea Journal*
   Carry a notebook with you and jot down any ideas that come up. Too often these ideas are dismissed as nonsense. The more you

acknowledge these ideas, the more ideas will show up, increasing your creativity. Go back and review your ideas. Is there a theme?

What will you explore later?

2. *Work Journal*

   Keep a notebook in the breakroom of your job and have staff write down things they are grateful for, acts of kindness, and observations they have. This can be related to Six Sigma projects, special initiatives, or a general practice. Review at a staff meeting or during a special meeting to discuss "Matters of the Heart" or the "Breakroom Conversation."

3. *Memory Book*

   Start a journal for your child, niece, or even a friend's baby and periodically write down what is happening, adding pictures and memorabilia. Have entries on the child's birthday, your birthday, and other special dates. Give it to the child on his or her sixth, tenth, or sixteenth birthday.

4. *Couple or Family Journal*

   Keep a journal in the kitchen and use this to communicate in happy times and especially during conflict. This can be used to focus on gratitude and family values and to reflect on the growth years.

5. *Reflection Journal*

Use a journal to reflect on major events, difficult experiences, both work and personal. Reflection increases self-confidence, builds skills, strengthens resilient thinking, and develops your interpersonal skills. This is a great journal to use when starting your mindfulness practice, presented next.

Reflection increases your effectiveness as a leader, in clinical practice, as a parent or in any relationship. Reflection will help you regulate your attention, improve concentration and make better decisions.

6. *Thought Journal*

With the right thoughts, there is nothing you cannot handle. This is the foundation of resilient thinking—having thoughts that are optimistic, realistic, and based in confidence. Keep a running log of your thoughts. Use your Day Timer and keep an inventory of your thoughts.

At the end of the day, review and reframe negative thoughts into positive ones. Notice any pattern? What triggers negative (or positive) thoughts?

Sound crazy? The most successful leaders do this to increase their awareness and control the most important tool they have—their mindset.

Tips for Journaling

1. Give yourself the space to be distraction-free. Turn off your phone, social media, and anything else that will interrupt you during your journaling.

2. Set a time limit and use your timer. Consistency is more effective than binge journaling. Staying true to your time limit will keep you focused and more likely to consistently journal.

3. Have a specific goal in mind for the journal session. This could be to reflect on a conversation you have had, how your day went, or to better understand your reaction to something. Define your intention for the journaling session.

4. Start this session with a few deep breaths on a count of four and inhale some essential oils. Citrus blends are uplifting, peppermint is stimulating, and lavender is relaxing. Make this part of the ritual.

5. You can use the computer and type or handwrite in a notebook. Many prefer writing it out and find this allows for a greater flow of ideas, thoughts, and emotions.

6. Be sure to date your entries.

7. Begin to write (or type), and do not censor or edit. Just write for five minutes. Then, read what you have written. Ask yourself, "What does this mean for me?" and further explore what you have written.

8. Keep your journal private.

9. Journaling can be especially powerful after difficult *as well as* happy times. You can also set up a weekly ritual to write.

10. This is not the time to be critical of your writing. No need to proof for grammar. Journaling is a release, a log of ideas or thoughts, or memories. This is not an essay, novel, or blog post. It is for your eyes only.

11. Go back and review your journal every quarter. Have you made progress? Why or why not? This gives you the opportunity to change course and take different steps to achieve your goal.

Chapter Summary: Mindset Reboot

- » Count of 4 breathing will immediately release tension. Use it throughout the day.

- » We tend to expend more energy than we renew. It is essential to use some type of stress strategy every day.

- » Practice some form of mindfulness every day to boost your focus and concentration.

- » Use the body scan to check in with yourself.

- » Journaling is a very effective way to relax your mind and prompt reflection. This increases your learning and application of what you've learned.

Study Group Activity

» Choose one of the strategies for the week. Encourage everyone in the group to use it.

» Discuss the difference it made for them.

Appendix

The following forms, along with many other checklists, on-the-go training and courses are available in the Work Smart Club Network.

www.worksmartclubnetwork.com

5 Why's

This simple technique produces powerful results. It originated in the 1930's as part of Toyota's "go and see" philosophy, where managers spent time on the shop floor to get to the root of problems. The technique is still used today.

This is helpful with simple to moderately difficult problems. Once you have your team in place, the process goes like this:

1. Observe the problem in action if possible. Define the problem, write it on a whiteboard.

2. Then ask Why?

Let's say the problem is:

There is a delay in the appointment times for new clients lowering customer satisfaction.

To answer the question, you want to think about what is happening and speak to the facts rather than make up potential reasons that this is happening. Let's go with this example:

Why? ▶ ▶ ▶ ▶ All new appointments are routed through the admissions department.

Why? ▶ ▶ ▶ ▶ So admissions will know how many new clients there are.

Why? ▶ ▶ ▶ ▶ The Admission manager is now in charge of this clinic.

Why? ▶ ▶ ▶ ▶ This was part of restructuring.

Why? ▶ ▶ ▶ ▶ The manager in charge was new and not familiar with the patient process.

Countermeasure:

Reroute calls back to clinic for faster service and report all new admissions every 4 hours.

3. Stop, when asking "why" no longer produces any useful information and you can go no further. It is not always 5 times. It could more or less.

4. Now that you have a root cause, your team comes up with countermeasures to solve the problem.

5. Monitor and measure the solution to be sure it continues to eliminate the root cause problem. You may need to adjust it to achieve the desired result.

Interruption Log

Keep this log for 3 days to 1 week. Are there patterns? Are you interrupting yourself?

Date/ Time	Interruption	Time Spent	Time to get Back to Previous	Did you lose focus?

Perfectionism Self Check & 360

Take the quiz. Any red flags? Give this sheet to someone you trust and ask them to rate you using this scale: 1 is almost never and 10 is all the time.

1. I have to be right.	1 2 3 4 5 6 7 8 9 10
2. I am very competitive.	1 2 3 4 5 6 7 8 9 10
3. I have a hard time making decisions/choices.	1 2 3 4 5 6 7 8 9 10
4. I am never satisfied.	1 2 3 4 5 6 7 8 9 10
5. I am critical of others.	1 2 3 4 5 6 7 8 9 10
6. I procrastinate.	1 2 3 4 5 6 7 8 9 10
7. I do not like to be criticized.	1 2 3 4 5 6 7 8 9 10
8. I feel guilty if I cannot follow through on something.	1 2 3 4 5 6 7 8 9 10
9. I am nervous about sharing my opinion.	1 2 3 4 5 6 7 8 9 10
10. If I make a mistake I feel like a failure.	1 2 3 4 5 6 7 8 9 10
11. I worry about what others think of me.	1 2 3 4 5 6 7 8 9 10
12. I have to stay busy to feel good about myself.	1 2 3 4 5 6 7 8 9 10
13. I am late because I needed to get something done.	1 2 3 4 5 6 7 8 9 10
14. It is hard to ask someone to do something because they will not do it as well as I would.	1 2 3 4 5 6 7 8 9 10

Add up the number

16 Dimensions on the EQi 2.0

The EQi 2.0, is the world's leading assessment on emotional intelligence; there are 16 dimensions (skill sets) on that assessment. See them below.

SELF-REGARD: Express your ideas, thoughts confidently and are comfortable in the process.

SELF-ACTUALIZATION: This is your ability to pursue meaningful goals and become the very best you can be.

EMOTIONAL SELF AWARENESS: This is the foundation of emotional intelligence. When you know what is going on inside, you can act intentionally and in line with your goals.

EMOTIONAL EXPRESSION: Do you express your emotions in a direct way that is appropriate in intensity, thoughtful, respectful and clear?

ASSERTIVENESS: Assertiveness is respectful, intentional and sensitive and it means you set limits, boundaries and state your position clearly and evenly.

INDEPENDENCE: It means you can work, think and act on your own and you can also be a team member when needed.

RELATIONSHIPS: This competency in EI is your ability to work with people in order to get the job done.

EMPATHY: A set of skills, both emotional and behavioral skills, that allows one to connect with, understand, and relate to another, in order to provide support.

SOCIAL RESPONSIBILITY: Your ability to align with values of the greater good.

PROBLEM SOLVING: Your ability to define the problem and find creative solutions. Too often, problems are not well defined, and initiatives fail.

REALITY TESTING: Increased awareness and insight into what you feel and how you see the world.

IMPULSE CONTROL: Your ability to delay gratification for the benefit of your goals.

FLEXIBILITY: Your ability to adapt, shift or adjust your behaviors, thoughts and emotions to what is required of you in the moment.

STRESS TOLERANCE: Resilience is your ability to bounce back from challenges without permanent damage.

OPTIMISM: Your ability to hold positive expectations, remain hopeful and resilient even in the face of challenge.

WELL-BEING: Your overall sense of satisfaction with yourself and your life.

When you take this assessment, we will establish your baseline, and using these dimensions, identify your natural leadership style.

Mindful Attention Worksheet

Jot down any situation that brought up feelings/ thoughts.

Indicate which emotion/ thought arose, how strong it was, and how you dealt with it.

Event	Emotions/ Thoughts it Brings Up: (Happy, Sad, Angry, Worried, Frustrated, Etc.)	Rate Feeling 5=Very Strong 1=Not Strong at All 5 4 3 2 1	How I Dealt with the Emotion:
Boss:			
Coworkers:			
Friends:			
Family:			
Other:			

The Work Smart Club Network

This is our online Center for Work and Well-being, a platform with training in resilience, emotional intelligence and problem solving. We include topics to help you get more done, balance work and life, strengthen your leadership, eliminate stress, and support your well-being.

We offer a library of premium resources with video, audio, templates, checklists, guidebooks and a monthly live coaching call.

Visit **www.worksmartclubmetwork.com**

About Work Smart Consulting

Work Smart Consulting provides executive and organizational development, consulting, and leadership training, utilizing Emotional Intelligence (Ei) tools and practices. We assess, coach, and train for resilient thinking using Ei, resilience strategies, and the Lean Six Sigma process.

Dr. Howard provides a variety of training options to build the skills leaders need to be more effective and enjoy their work-life.

> Contact us today and schedule a complimentary session to find out what program is best for you and your work group.

Here is what one participant has said:

"This program changed my life. I have concrete tools I can use with my team, and I have finally learned to honor my strengths. This confidence takes the struggle out of my day since I no longer have to second guess myself."

—Danielle F., DNP, Director of Emergency Services

About the Author

Cynthia Howard RN, PhD, LSSBB is an Executive Coach and Performance Consultant and helps professionals, leaders, and executives master their mindset and their attention for consistent success.

Cynthia is a mentor, coach, and resilience champion, and in the past twenty-plus years, she has coached thousands of individuals to consistently perform at a high level for greater success and fulfillment.

Dr. Cynthia integrates the latest research in the fields of flow, resilience, emotional intelligence, and high performance within the structure of Lean and Six sigma. This combination offers rapid, lasting change.

Black belt in Lean Sigma | Fellow in AIS | Licensed Heartmath Trainer and Coach

To contact Cynthia about this program, speaking at your organization, or for a consultation to use lean principles email drh@worksmartthinkdifferent.com

www.worksmartthinkdifferent.com

Other Books Written by Dr. Cynthia Howard

The Work Smart Principle
Leadership Leverage Through Faith and Focus

EVERYDAY EMOTIONAL INTELLIGENCE
Fatal Emotions, Drama, Conflict, Bullying... A Guide to Better Communication

105 Tips to Work Smart

365 Power Thoughts: The Mindset Difference

HEAL: Healthy Emotions. Abundant Life.
From Superhero to Super Self-Empowered. Master your Emotional Intelligence.

References

American Nurses Credentialing Center (2006). "Benefits of becoming a magnet-designated facility." <http://www.nursingworld.org/ancc/magnet/benes.html>.

Argyris, C. (1990). *Overcoming Organizational Defenses: Facilitating Organizational Learning.* Jossey Bass: San Francisco.

Bass, B. M. (1985). *Leadership and Performance.* New York, NY: Free Press. Needham, MA: Allyn & Bacon.

Burns, J. M. (1978). *Leadership.* New York, NY: Harper and Row.

Barrios-Choplin, Bob, PhD, McCraty, Rollin, Ph.D., Sundram, Joseph, M.Ed. and Atkinson, Mike (1999). "The Effect of Employee Self-Management Training on Personal and Organizational Quality." HeartMath Research Center, Institute of HeartMath. Publication No. 99-083. Boulder Creek, CA.

Barrios-Choplin, Bob, PhD, McCraty, Rollin, PhD, Cryer, Bruce, MA. (1997). "An inner quality approach to reducing stress and improving physical and emotional well-being at work." *Stress Medicine.* Vol. 13. 193–201.

Branham, L. (205). The 7 Hidden Reasons Employees Leave. Amacom: New York.

Carr, N. (2011) *The Shallows: What the Internet Is Doing to Our Brains.* W.W. Norton: New York

Chermis, C., Goleman, D. (2001). *The Emotionally Intelligent Workplace.* San Francisco: Jossey Bass.

Covey, S. (2004). *The 7 Habits of Highly Effective People: Powerful Lessons in Personal Change.* New York: Free Press.

Csikszentmihalyi, M. (1990) *Flow: the Psychology of Optimal Experience.* Harper Perennial: New York

Duhigg, C. (2012) *The Power of Habit. Why We Do What We Do In Life and Business.* Random House: New York.

Dweck, C. (2008) Mindset: The New Psychology of Success. Random house: New York.

EQi 2.0 Workplace Report (2011). Multi Health Systems.

Erickson, R., & Grove, W. (2007, October). "Why emotions matter: Age, agitation, and burnout among registered nurses." *Online Journal of Issues in Nursing.* 13(1).

Feinstein, D. (2008a). Energy psychology: a review of the preliminary evidence. *Psychotherapy: Theory, Research, Practice, Training.* 45(2), 199–213.

Fromm, Erich (1956). *The Art of Loving*. Harper and Row.

Gallup (2016). Q 12 - Meta-analysis report. The Relationship Between Engagement at Work and Organizational Outcomes. Ninth Edition.

Gardner, H. (2011). *Frames of Mind: The Theory of Multiple Intelligences*. Basic Books: New York.

Goleman, D. (1995). Emotional Intelligence and Why It Matters More than IQ. New York: Bantam Books.

Holt, Jim. "Time Bandits: What were Einstein and Gödel talking about?" *New Yorker*, February 28, 2005.

Horwath, R. (2014). *Elevate: The Three Disciplines of Advanced Strategic Thinking*. New Jersey: John Wiley and Sons.

Howard, Cynthia (2012). "Use This Simple Tool to Transform Your Stress and Avoid Nursing Burnout. Part 1 and 2." *NurseTogether*. <http://www.nursetogether.com/Lifestyle/Lifestyle-Article>.

Howard, Cynthia (2015). *HEAL: Healthy Emotions. Abundant Life. From Super Hero To Super Self Empowered*. Florida: Vibrant Radiant Health.

Iacoboni, M. (2009) *Mirroring People: The New Science of How We Connect with Others*. Picador: New York.

Mehrabian, A. (1972). *Silent Messages: Implicit Communication of Emotions and Attitudes*. Wadsworth Publishing Company.

Patterson, K., Grenney, J., McMillan, R., Switzler, A., Maxfield, D. (2013). *Crucial Accountability: Tools for Resolving Violated Expectations, Broken Commitments, and Bad Behavior.* McGraw Hill.

Pentland, A. The Science of Building Great Teams. Harvard Business Review. April 2012.

Rath, T., Harter, J. (2010). Well Being: The 5 Essential Elements. Gallup Press.

Robison, J. "The Business Case for Wellbeing." Business Journal. 9 June 2010.

Rozin, P., & Royzman, E. "Negativity bias, negativity dominance, and contagion". Personality and Social Psychology Review, 5, 2001. 296-320.

Rubik B. (2002). The biofield hypothesis: Its biophysical basis and role in medicine. *Journal of Alternative and Complementary Medicine*, 8:703–717.

Seligman, M. (1991). *Learned Optimism: How to Change Your Mind and Your Life.* New York: Vintage Books.

Seligman, M. (2011). *Flourish: A Visionary New Understanding of Happiness and Well-being.* New York: Free Press.

Silow-Carroll, Sharon, Alteras, Tanya, & Meyer, Jack A. (2007, April). "Hospital quality improvement: Strategies and lessons from U.S. hospitals." *Health Management Associates.*

Stallard, M. (2015). *Connection Culture.* VA: ATD Press.

Stein, Steven J., & Book, Howard E. *The EQ edge: Emotional intelligence and your success.* Ontario, Canada: Jossey Bass. 211.

Stone, D., Heen, S. (2015). *Thanks for Providing Feedback: The Science and Art of Receiving Feedback Well.* New York: Penguin Books.

Sy T., Cote S., Saavedra R. (2005). "The Contagious Leader: Impact of the Leader's Mood on the Mood of Group Members, Group Affective Tone, and Group Processes." *Journal of Applied Psychology*, 2005. Vol. 90, No. 2, 295–305.

Thompson, Henry (2010). *The Stress Effect.* San Francisco, CA: Jossey Bass.

Endnotes

[1] Iso-Ahola, S. E., & Dotson, C. O. (2016). Psychological Momentum-A Key to Continued Success. Frontiers in psychology, 7, 1328. doi:10.3389/fpsyg.2016.01328

[2] Gallup (2016). Q 12 - Meta-analysis report. The Relationship Between Engagement at Work and Organizational Outcomes. Ninth Edition.

[3] Hausknecht, J. "What Predicts Executive Success," http://www.amanet.org/training/articles/New-Study-Shows-Nice-Guys-Finish-First.aspx?pcode=XCRP

[4] Herbert, Beate & Pollatos, Olga. (2012). The Body in the Mind: On the Relationship Between Interoception and Embodiment. Topics in cognitive science. 4. 692-704.

[5] Kaplan, R., Norton, D. (2005) The Office of Strategy Management. Harvard Business Review. October.

[6] Clance, P. R. (1985). *The Impostor Phenomenon: When Success Makes You Feel Like A Fake.* Toronto: Bantam Books.

See also Clance, Pauline Rose; Imes, Suzanne A. (1978). "The imposter phenomenon in high achieving women: Dynamics and therapeutic intervention." (PDF). *Psychotherapy: Theory, Research & Practice* 15 (3): 241–247.

[7] McCraty, R., Atkinson, M., Tomasino, D. (2001) *Science of the Heart.* Overview of Research Conducted by the Institute of Heartmath. Boulder, CO.

[8] McCraty, R., Atkinson, M., Tomasino, D., & Bradley, R. T, The coherent heart: Heart-brain interactions, psychophysiological coherence, and the emergence of system-wide order. *Integral Review*, 2009. 5(2): p. 10-115.

[9] Carr, N. (2011) *The Shallows: What the Internet Is Doing to Our Brains.* W.W. Norton: New York

[10] Helfley, C. *Kanban Roadmap: How to Get Started in 5 Easy Steps.* A Guide from Leankit. E-book.

[11] Babcock, L., Laschever, S. (2007). *Women Don't Ask: The High Cost of Avoiding Negotiation—and Positive Strategies for Change.* Bantam Books.

[12] Southwick, S., Charney, D. (2012). Resilience: The Science of Mastering Life's Greatest Challenges. New York: University of Cambridge Press.

[13] Seligman, M. (1991*). Learned Optimism: How to Change Your Mind and Your Life.* New York: Vintage Books.

[14] Ellis, L. (2012). *Leading with Honor: Leadership Lessons from the Hanoi Hilton.* Freedom Star Press.

[15] Damasio, A. (2000) *The Feeling of What Happens: Body and Emotion in the Making of Consciousness.* Mariner Books.

[16] Mehrabian, A. (1972). Silent Messages: Implicit Communication of Emotions and Attitudes. Wadsworth Publishing Company.

www.ingramcontent.com/pod-product-compliance
Lightning Source LLC
Chambersburg PA
CBHW071354290426
44108CB00014B/1548